The Beginner's Guide to

Content Marketing for Small Businesses

The **Beginner's Guide** to **Content Marketing** for **Small Businesses**

1. Understand content marketing basics so you can decide whether it's right for your business

2. Take your first steps toward creating great content

3. Discover where you can learn more about content marketing and find help

Matt Mansfield

www.mattsmansfield.com

Matt About Business, LLC, 1520 Woodbine Court, Deerfield, IL 60015

http://www.1000contentideas.com

Quantity (Bulk) Sales:

Special discounts are available on quantity purchases. For details, contact the publisher at either one of the addresses above.

First Edition: June, 2014
ISBN: 978-0-9888437-0-7

Library of Congress Control Number: 2014908956

Table of Contents

INTRODUCTION

This book was supposed to be a lot longer.

When I first sat down to write, I had 32 chapters and 5 appendices all planned out in one slick-looking outline. It took me almost a year of writing to discover the error inherent in my approach; an error that I'd like to share in a quick content marketing lesson.

A Quick Content Marketing Lesson

Whether read, listened-to or watched, content needs to be consumed by your target customers to be effective. To increase the likelihood of that consumption, your content's topic, information and design must take your target customer into account, something that I initially failed to do in this case.

You see, the target customer for this book is people who market a small business online. Being part of a small business, these people likely wears many hats besides marketing such as serving customers, planning, getting things done and so forth. In other words, these people are very busy.

> A content marketing lesson in the introduction? Well, what can I say, it's just one indication of how value-packed this book truly is.

So what crazy idea made me think they'd have time to read a book with 32 chapters and 5 appendices?!

Error realized, I grabbed my machete and trimmed the book down to a much more manageable five chapters and two appendices. What's left is the tightly focused book you hold in your hand.

Did I waste a year writing pages that will never see the light of day? As if! The content trimmed (or should I say hacked?) from this book is being converted into both online courses and eBooks that will show why, how, when and where to create and use the many types of content including blog posts, videos, podcasts, infographics, webinars and much more. Each course and eBook will be easy to understand, provide actionable steps and advice and include plenty of examples.

These offerings will be a perfect complement this book. Building on the knowledge found within these pages, both courses and eBooks will enable you to plan, create and implement increasingly effective content marketing campaigns.

And that's a good thing.

To stay up-to-date on my latest course and eBook offerings, make sure to visit my "Learn with Me" page online at http://bit.ly/1n6FafB regularly.

What This Book Will Help You Do

This book will help you complete three important tasks:

Understand Content Marketing Basics so You Can Decide Whether It's Right for Your Business

The aim of the first three chapters is to bring you to a point where you can make an informed decision on whether content marketing should be added to your marketing mix or not. We'll discuss the history and definition of content marketing, the benefits of using content marketing and how to figure out if your business should use content marketing.

Take Your First Steps Toward Creating Great Content

If you determine that content marketing is a good fit for your business, then the aim of the following two chapters is to lay the foundation of content creation. We'll discuss what goes into creating great content and how to get past the most common hurdles.

Discover Where You Can Learn More About Content Marketing and Find Help

The aim of the two appendices is to support you as you take your first steps into content marketing. We'll discuss why, where and how to hire outside help such as an agency or freelancer and where to go online to learn much more about implementing an effective content marketing campaign.

A Quick Note About the Web Addresses (URLs) in this Book

Many of the links contained in this book were shortened to make them easier for you to use. When entering these links into your browser's address bar, it's important to copy them exactly as they appear in the book using both upper and lower case characters.

I'd Like to Thank...

Writing a book is hard. Even for those of us who create content every day, it quickly becomes clear that books are an entirely different beast than other types of content such as posts, infographics, videos or webinars. Luckily, I've had tons of help getting through this herculean task so before we move on to the rest of the book, I'd like to send my thanks to those who helped me along the way.

Front and center, I'd like to send a huge thanks to both Nicole Fende, my book shepherd and Monette Satterfield, my copyeditor. Without your excellent advice, skills, encouragement and infinite patience this book would never have been born. Thank you, thank you, thank you!

In the, "Keeping Matt Going" category, I'd like to thank Brooke Kayman Fox for keeping me sane throughout this project and Laura Petrolino for her eternal optimism.

Thanks to my two sisters Lisa Mansfield and Janet Seide; the former for listening and the latter for helping me realize that finishing this book was the only step I can take *right now* to achieve my goals.

Last but certainly not least, I'd like to thank my wife Mimi and dad Morris for the support they've provided in so many ways and over such a long time. You two are my anchors and I love ya' both!!!

SECTION I: Understand Content Marketing Basics so You Can Decide Whether It's Right for Your Business

The aim of the first three chapters is to bring you to a point where you can make an informed decision on whether content marketing should be added to your marketing mix or not. We'll discuss three topics:

1) The history and definition of content marketing;

2) The benefits of using content marketing; and

3) How to figure out if your business should use content marketing.

Chapter 1: What is Content Marketing?

Like most advances, content marketing isn't a revolutionary idea; it's an evolutionary idea. Fueled by the need to attract target customers in a noisy marketplace as well as advances in affordable and easy-to-use technology, content marketing has quickly become one of the most effective ways to sell both products and services online.

In this chapter, we're going to take a look at how content marketing came to be. After that we'll dig into the core goal of marketing – an important step in preparing you to attack the concepts and ideas we'll be covering throughout the rest of the book.

In the Beginning, There Was Outbound Marketing

From the time stall owners called out to customers in open-air marketplaces, outbound marketing tactics have aimed to catch a customer's attention by interrupting what they are currently doing (that's why outbound marketing is also called "Interruption Marketing").

> Outbound marketing tactics catch a customer's attention by interrupting what they're doing.

Imagine a target customer:

- Happily watching a television show when all of a sudden, it is interrupted by commercials.
- Enjoying a magazine when all of a sudden seven subscription cards fall out at once.
- Tanning on the beach when all of a sudden the sun is blocked by a huge advertising blimp.

Annoying, eh? Well yes, but very, very effective.

This is the kind of marketing that has dominated from the first day a seller called out in a marketplace up until the present day. That's right; almost all the marketing methods you're familiar with are outbound including:

- Television, radio and print advertisements and sponsorships;
- Direct mail;
- Mail-order catalogs;
- Public relations;
- Online banners and advertisements;
- People wearing placards and walking around town to attract customers;
- Pay-per-click advertisements on search engines and social media sites;
- Employees handing out packets of tissues that advertise a business (this is a Japanese approach - yeah, I like manga and anime); and
- Telemarketing calls.

Each of these methods seeks to grab a customer's attention by interrupting them while they're going about their everyday life. Once a seller has a customer's attention, they deliver a call to action such as, "Go buy a car at an authorized dealer - 0% financing" or "Come visit our restaurant for a great meal - $10 off if you bring this coupon."

Is Outbound Marketing Bad?

Outbound marketing isn't inherently evil, but it's gotten a bad reputation. I mean, who wants to be interrupted when they're doing something else?

However, the biggest downside of outbound marketing, especially for small businesses, is cost. It costs money to reach out to your customers and the more customers you want to reach, the more money you have to spend.

Just look at the price of Super Bowl ads.

Another downside is that technology is making it harder to interrupt folks. Now, Digital Video Recorders (DVRs) let you skip commercials, digital magazines let you skip all those subscription cards and satellite radio is practically commercial-free.

However, outbound marketing works well. If you have the cash, it's an approach that can drive your target customers to action. As a business, you shouldn't dismiss outbound marketing out of hand – it can complement a content marketing campaign quite well so it's wise to consider interruption tactics when developing an integrated marketing campaign.

Just because an approach is an oldie, doesn't mean it's not a goodie!

Inbound Marketing a.k.a. Content Marketing

As opposed to the interruption tactics of outbound marketing, inbound marketing tries to catch a customer's attention by helping them with what they're already doing. With this approach, your marketing campaigns don't interrupt customers; they help them answer questions such as:

> Inbound marketing tactics catch a customer's attention by helping them with what they're already doing.

- What products or services can help me solve a problem or meet a need?
- What are the features of this product or service?
- Which version of product or level of service will best fit my needs?
- How do I get the most out of my product or service once I've bought it?

Inbound marketing is mostly about information and that's why it's called content marketing.

Why content? Because creating content such as text, images, audio and video and publishing them on your blog and on social sharing sites can help answer your customer's questions and solve their problems. The benefits of doing so are huge and we'll discuss them in more detail in Chapter 2.

You might ask, "If it's so great, why haven't businesses used content marketing up until now?" The answer is that is until recently, content marketing wasn't a viable marketing tactic. You couldn't be right where your customers were whenever they had a question (that would be expensive *and* creepy) so they couldn't find you and your wonderful products and services when they needed you. However, since 1990 there's been one affordable spot where your target customers can find you 24 hours a day, 7 days a week (24x7 from now on): the Internet.

The Internet's Role in Content Marketing

Thanks to technology, the marketing tactics that began with a stall owner's call in an open-air marketplace have expanded to print, radio, television and the Internet.

The latest stage, the Internet (or World Wide Web or just the Web – I'll call it all three throughout the book) has made content marketing possible.

Here's how it works (Image 2.1):

1. Create content to answer your target customers' questions:
   a. Text such as blog posts, articles, white papers and presentations;
   b. Images including photos and infographics;
   c. Audio podcasts and online radio; and
   d. Videos that are educational and entertaining.
2. Publish the content on your site.
3. Post links to your content at other media outlets (e.g. YouTube, Slideshare, Pinterest, etc.).

4. Customers find the links to your content from searches at sites like Google and social sharing sites like Twitter, Facebook and LinkedIn.

5. Customers follow the links back to your site where they learn about you and your products and services.

Best of all, this can happen 24x7 so you're able to be there when your customers need you.

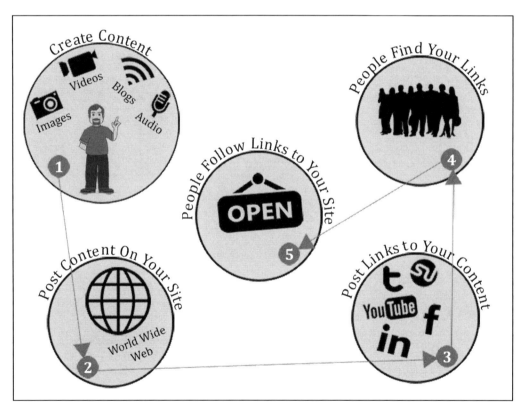

Image 2.1: A High-Level Overview of the Content Marketing Process.

These types of content creation steps couldn't take place without the Web. Sure, you could create content before the Web existed, but not such a broad range of engaging and useful formats. Before the Web, the cost of publishing and distributing your content to target customers was prohibitive and that put content marketing well out the reach of most businesses, especially small ones.

What about links? Without the Web, links wouldn't exist and neither would a centralized search system nor a way to easily share content (my mother used to mail articles to me – stamp, envelope and all – but it would take an army of folks to do the same for your business).

> Without the Web, your target customers would have a much more difficult time finding your business.

Without the Web, your target customers would have a much more difficult time finding you and learning about your products and services. They certainly wouldn't have 24x7 access to you - you gotta' sleep sometime – and it costs a lot to have someone else answering your phone overnight. Now, with the World Wide Web, all of the steps that make up content marketing are possible. Even better, they're affordable and within the reach of any size business – a handy fact for small businesses that want to achieve the core goal of marketing.

The Core Goal of Marketing

Marketing has existed since the first time someone had a product or service to sell. Since that day the core goal of marketing has remained the same:

To capture a target customer's attention and
drive them to take action.

Capturing a Target Customer

Marketing is most effective when it's targeted at the person who is most likely to buy the product or service being marketed. That seems pretty obvious, but the effect on your bottom-line can be huge. It's one of the cardinal truths of marketing: "The less you spend to make each sale, the more money your business will make." Powerful stuff right there.

Targeting a customer consists of two elements:

1. Identifying the customers who are most likely to buy your products and services; and

2. Marketing to them with the words, images, videos, etc. that will drive them to take action.

> Marketing is most effective when it's targeted at the person who is most likely to buy the product or service being marketed.

Even back when stall vendors sold products in open-air marketplaces, target marketing was an everyday tactic.

- "Pretty lady, beautiful jewelry for a beautiful woman!"
- "Strong soldier, new blades with an edge that can cut armor like butter!"

OK, I admit to reading way too many fantasy novels, but you get my point. The best use of your marketing dollars is to target the person who is most likely to buy your products and using the words, images, videos, etc. that are most likely to drive them to take action.

> Targeting is especially essential for small businesses because they typically don't have much money to spend on marketing.

Targeting is especially essential for small

businesses because they typically don't have much money to spend on marketing. Every dollar needs to count. Targeting the most likely customers is the best way to ensure those dollars matter and we're going to discuss that many times throughout the book.

Targeting Your Customers Using Avatars

Each time you undertake all the marketing activities surrounding a specific offer, event, product and service, you should identify the folks that the campaign will target. You do this by creating one or more profiles of the type of people who are most likely to buy your products and services. You can have more than one target group per campaign so you may have more than one profile. Each of these profiles is called an "avatar".

An avatar can be simple or complex, depending on your targeting needs. You can learn more about customer avatars by following the links on my resource page at: http://bit.ly/1h3YB0r. For now, here's a sample of the specific information that might be used when creating an avatar:

- Gender
- Place They Live
- Height
- Job

- Age
- Education Level
- Marital Status
- Sites They Like

- Annual Income
- Weight
- Family Size
- Previous Purchase History

Once you have your avatars in hand, they should guide every step of your content marketing campaign, from the types of content you create to where you publish it online.

That's a key point. While targeting is powerful, it only works if you market in the spots where your target customers hang out. Having a presence online where your customers will be, and when, is a critical element of content marketing. For example:

1) If your target customers search for certain information online, your content must show up in those search results.

2) If your target customers look at certain sites for information, you should place your content on those sites.

Drive Them to Take Action

Marketing is useless if it doesn't drive your target customers to take action.

That said, the action you want a customer to take varies from campaign to campaign (and sometimes within a campaign!). Some of the actions you want your target customers to take include:

> Marketing is useless if it doesn't drive your target customers to take action.

- Buying a product or service;
- Telling others about your products or services;
- Signing-up for a newsletter or some other form of communication;
- Thinking better of your business because you sponsored an important cause; and
- Participating in a survey or some other market research activity.

Driving your target customers to take action can be critical to the survival of your business. Why? Just ask yourself - how long can you stay in business if no one buys any of your products?

How to Drive Action

If you've created your target customer avatars correctly, you've already done a large part of the work to drive action. That's because the customers you target with your marketing should be more willing to take action than other folks. Why? Because they are predisposed to want the products and services you're selling - after all, they *are* your most likely customers!

How do you get your target customers all the way to the next step - the one where they actually do something? Luckily, there are plenty of ways to encourage your target customers to take the next step. They are referred to as "Calls to Action".

> Drive your customers to take the next step with "Calls to Action".

Calls to Action

A call to action can take many forms and there is both a science and an art to creating them effectively (find helpful links to call to action resources at: http://bit.ly/1hJKGld). A few examples of calls to action are

- Offering a limited-time discount such as a coupon;
- Holding a sale around an event ("We just launched our new product!") or the calendar ("Spooky Halloween Sale!") or for any other reason you can think of ("My kid's an honor roll student!" sale); and

- Creating and posting a newsletter sign-up form on your site to capture leads and build an e-mail list that can be used to keep your business top-of-mind.

No matter how you entice your target customers to take action, there are a few important tips that will help.

Call to Action Tip #1

When you create your calls to action, keep your avatars in mind. Ask yourself, "What would motivate this avatar to take action?" The answer to that question may vary from avatar to avatar.

For example, Avatar-1 might be extremely motivated by the chance to save money while Avatar-2 couldn't care less. However, if you offer an opportunity to get the latest gadget before anyone else does, Avatar-2 will jump into action.

Call to Action Tip #2

Whether it's part of your website, a magazine ad, a direct mailer or a social media update, you should use as few calls to action in a single spot as you can, preferably just one. That's because too many calls to actions can confuse your customers, causing them to walk away without taking any action at all.

Be as clear as you can when you ask for an action. Give them one specific thing to do, and they'll be much more likely to take the action that you request.

Wash-Rinse-Repeat

Before we move on, there's one final fact you should understand:

Marketing is not an exact science.

It takes time to get a successful marketing strategy up and running. Even though you've created avatars and crafted compelling calls to action, you don't know how it will work in the real world until you try it.

> It takes time to get a successful marketing strategy up and running.

That's why this section is titled, "Wash-Rinse-Repeat." Over time, your marketing process will look like this:

1. Create your avatars.
2. Craft your calls to action.
3. Design and develop your marketing materials, online and off.
4. Launch your marketing campaign.
5. Test and measure the results (for online resources that will help you measure and test your content marketing efforts, visit: http://bit.ly/1eJykKx).
6. Use those measurements to see where to improve.
7. Back to step one.

This isn't to say that you can't hit your marketing goals out of the ballpark on your first go, but most often you won't and that's OK! If you spend too much time getting everything right, you'll never get to launch your product or service to the world. And, even then, there's no guarantee that it will work exactly as you planned.

Many small business folks get trapped at this stage in what's called "Analysis Paralysis" which is the inability to act before every single piece is in place and perfect. If you find yourself here, just go for it and take your best shot at creating your marketing strategy. When it feels right in your gut, go ahead and launch the campaign.

If it doesn't work as well as you hoped, that's ok. Take what you've learned and head back to the drawing board to try again.

You're Ready to Move On

Now that you understand how and why content marketing came about, as well as the core goal of marketing, it's time to take a look at the benefits that content marketing provides. These benefits extend well beyond being found online and their far-reaching effects can be surprising.

Onwards to chapter 2!

Chapter 2: Why Use Content Marketing?

In the last chapter, you learned about the goals of marketing in general and the evolution of marketing tactics from a voice calling out in a marketplace to inbound marketing using the World Wide Web. This chapter will take you on a deep dive into the benefits of using content marketing so you'll understand why it's fast becoming the hottest way to market your business online.

> This chapter will take you on a deep dive into the benefits of using content marketing.

The Core Goal of Content Marketing

The core goal of content marketing is:

To **drive targeted traffic** to your website **month-after-month** while **building authority, goodwill and trust**.

Let's break this down into the three main parts and learn how they work together.

Drive Targeted Traffic

There's nothing more frustrating than spending time, money and effort to build a business website that nobody ever visits. Unfortunately, many folks are frustrated with this experience. According to Wordtracker's keyword tool (www.wordtracker.com), in an average month, *more than 2,000,000* online searches are run for some variation of the phrase "how to get site traffic." Sadly, many of those searches are not at all helpful. You can avoid this frustration by using content marketing to attract website traffic. In fact, *77% of those surveyed reported that content marketing has helped increase their traffic.*[1] How does content marketing increase your online visibility and drive traffic? It's a two-part answer: search engines and casting your net to extend the reach of your content.

Search Engines

When someone visits a search engine like Google, they're searching for something, whether it's information, products, services or some combination of things. Search engine companies want to help searchers find what they want as quickly and easily as possible. Their goal is to make using their search engine so useful that folks return again and again to conduct more searches.

Why are search engine companies so interested in repeat customers? The answer to that question is **advertising**. When search engine companies present their search results, they also include ads on the page (Image 2.1).

These ads are the primary source of income for search engine companies. Every time a searcher clicks on an ad, the search engine company is paid a small fee by the business that placed the ad. That means search engine companies want as many people as possible to use their search engine because more searches mean more chances for people to click on the ads.

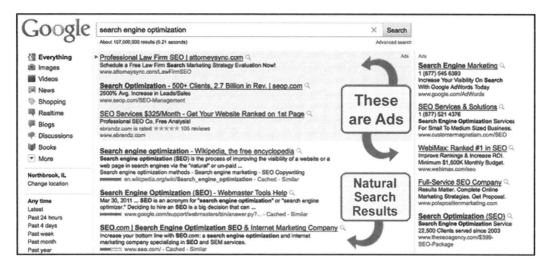

Image 2.1: Typical search engine results page.

How does content marketing fit into the picture? To get more people to use their search engine, the search engine company wants to make sure that searchers are happy with the results. To do that, search engine companies continually strive to make sure that the "natural search results" (labeled in Image 2.1) help folks quickly and easily find the information they're looking for. To do that, search engines must index quality content in their search database. And, because natural link results cannot be purchased like ads, this is where content marketers come into play.

By creating useful and entertaining content, content marketers are providing the information searchers are looking for. Therefore, search

> By creating content, content marketers enable search engine companies to provide useful search results to their searchers.

engine companies will rank a business with useful content higher causing their site listings to appear closer to the top of the natural search results. In turn, this results in more traffic to the content marketer's site. Of course, there's more to it than that, such as incoming links from other sites and Google authorship and authority, however, that discussion lies beyond the scope of this book (for a thorough overview of search engine optimization basics, check out my recorded webinar "SEO in Everyday English" at: http://bit.ly/1cHUrdO). For now, let's focus on the basic reason why content marketing plays so well with search engines and helps drive more traffic to your website. Nothing demonstrates that point better than a few real world statistics from a recent survey:

71% of those surveyed reported content marketing has helped them gain higher rankings in the search engines. [2]

Casting Your Net

Casting Your Net (CYN) is a term I like to use to describe a group of content marketing tactics that greatly extend the reach of your content. By using the CYN tactics, you'll expose your content to a larger audience of target customers and drive even more traffic to your website. The key to CYN is placing your content online where your target customers hang out. This targeted exposure increases the chance that they'll see your content and follow a link to your site. Some examples of CYN include:

> The key to casting your net is placing your content online where your target customers hang out.

- Posting links to your content in relevant online communities, forums and article sites that your target customers visit and social media networks such as Twitter, Facebook, YouTube, Pinterest, and LinkedIn;
- Writing guest posts and other content to be posted on sites other than your own that your target customers visit; and
- Using E-mail marketing to create links to content with scheduled e-mails that folks have signed up for.

Posting Links to Your Content

No matter what type of business you run, there are many online communities and forums that cater to the same audience as yours. Many of those sites have a place for you to share relevant content and share links back to your site. For instance, my target audience is the small-to-medium business community. There are many sites that serve this community and many of them have created just such a spot to share. I add links to my site every time I publish new content to these sites. Here are three that I use frequently.

1. **BizSugar** - http://www.bizsugar.com
2. **Bloomberg Current** - http://bloombergcurrent.com
3. **LinkedIn Groups -** http://www.linkedin.com

In addition to online communities and forums, article sites such as EzineArticles (http://ezinearticles.com) will publish your content for other people to use on their own sites. The benefit to you: when other folks post your content, it includes a short bio and link back to your site. Last, social media sites such as Twitter, Facebook and LinkedIn are excellent places to share links to your content and will drive even more traffic to your site.

Guest Posts

Guest posting is the creation of content to be published on a website other than your own. Typically, your content is accompanied by a short bio and a link back to your site (Image 2.2).

About the author: Matt Mansfield is a recognized expert in online business and the President of Matt About Business where he helps entrepreneurs and Fortune 500 companies figure out what their business SHOULD be doing online.

This article is from the SmallBizLady special blog series: 31 Ways to Boost Your Small Business in 2013. #Boost2013

Image 2.2: My bio and a link from one of my guest posts.

The two biggest content marketing benefits to guest posting are:

1. Your content appears on a site with more traffic than yours which exposes your business to more of your target customers, and

2. By posting your content on their site, the site owner is in essence endorsing you, which can lead to more trust - which is really important (more on that a little later in the chapter).

E-Mail Marketing

E-mail marketing is a great way to CYN out to your target customers using their very own inbox. The best part of e-mail marketing is that subscribers have already signed up to receive your e-mails (if not, you're spamming, so stop it!). Taking the time and effort to sign up means they're truly interested in what you have to say and share and that's a good thing.

Why is that? Because your subscribers' interest means they're warm prospects that are more likely to take action on offers you make in your e-mails.

> E-mail marketing is a great way to cast your net out to your target customers using their very own inbox.

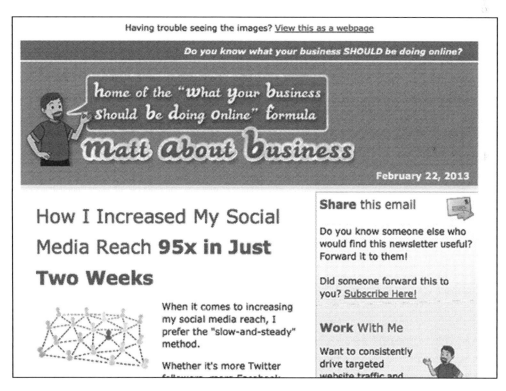

Image 2.3: One of my Matt About Business e-mail newsletters.

A Note on the Targeted part of "Drive Targeted Traffic"

Remember, even if your site gets a lot of traffic, it all goes to waste if it's not targeted. As we covered in Chapter 1, you want to attract traffic that consists of the folks who are most likely to buy your products and services. If done correctly, content marketing will drive targeted traffic, from both search engines and from CYN tactics. Since it's so important, let's go

> Even if your site gets a lot of traffic, it all goes to waste if that traffic isn't targeted.

over our core goal again before we move on to its second part. The core goal of content marketing is:

To **drive targeted traffic** to your website **month-after-month**
while **building authority, goodwill and trust**.

Month-After-Month

One of the most significant areas in which content marketing beats the pants off of outbound marketing is in return-on-investment (ROI). ROI is a measure of what you get out minus what you put in. For this book, ROI can be calculated with this equation:

> Content marketing beats the pants off of outbound marketing in terms of ROI.

(Total sales dollars – Total marketing dollars spent to get the sales)
\ Total marketing dollars spent to get the sales) = ROI%

A higher ROI percentage means more profit. Also, as you can see in the equation above, the less you spend on marketing, the higher your ROI will be. So why does content marketing return a higher ROI than outbound marketing? It has to do with the amount of money you spend to make your sales.

Outbound Marketing and ROI

In Chapter 1 we learned that one of the biggest downsides to outbound marketing is the cost. To make a sale with outbound marketing, you must continually interrupt your target customers and attract their attention. This means that you need to continue spending marketing dollars every month in order to keep making sales. Whether you spend money on offline print and television advertisements or on online pay-per-click advertisements, over time the cost of ongoing marketing is a drag on your profits. Until recently, outbound tactics were the standard marketing approach and folks accepted the higher costs of sales as part of doing business. The arrival of content marketing changed all that.

> Until content marketing came along, folks accepted the higher costs of outbound marketing sales as part of doing business.

Content Marketing and ROI

When you create a piece of content and publish it on the Internet, you only do it once and only incur the cost once. However, that piece of content can bring people to your site long after it was published. That means you'll spend less to attract the attention of more target customers. This "spend once, get targeted traffic for a long time" effect has increased the ROI of marketing online dramatically. One study found that **leads from inbound marketing cost on average 61% less than outbound marketing leads.** [3]

Let's take a closer look at this idea. I'm going to share some real life numbers from my Matt About Business blog on December 14, 2012. These numbers will demonstrate how long one piece of paid-for-once content can continue to attract traffic over time.

> The "spend once, get targeted traffic for a long time" effect has increased the ROI of marketing online dramatically

Selected Real-Life Content Marketing Results

Notes:

1. All numbers are 2012 year-to-date as of December 14, 2012.

2. Numbers do not reflect additional traffic from search engines other than Google or traffic from social media networks; however, much of that traffic was also the result of my content marketing efforts.

3. All Google searches results numbers were calculated using the "Currently hiding personal results" setting (see the box on page 26 for more info about personal results).

Post: 2 Simple Steps to Find a Manufacturer for Your Product Online	
Link: http://bit.ly/1img3SB	

Published: November 18, 2010 – (over 2 years prior to the numbers below!)	
Statistic	2012 Number
Unique Visitors Overall	3,965 people
Average Time on Page Overall	50 minutes, 33 seconds
Unique Visitors from Google	3,408 people
Average Time on Page for Google Visitors	55 minutes, 47 seconds
Google Search Term	Ranking on Google Search Results
how to find a manufacturer	5th out of 719,000,000 results

Post: 1000+ Content Ideas for Your Blog or Newsletter	
Link: http://bit.ly/1eEIk7T	

Published: November 18, 2011 – (over 1 year prior to the numbers below!)	
Statistic	2012 Number
Unique Visitors Overall	1,695 people
Average Time on Page Overall	25 minutes, 46 seconds
Unique Visitors from Google	1,348 people
Average Time on Page for Google Visitors	34 minutes, 43 seconds
Google Search Term	Ranking on Google Search
business newsletter ideas	4th out of 710,000,000 results
newsletter content ideas	4th out of 230,000,000 results

The "Personal Results" feature changes the way your search results are returned on Google. If you're logged onto Google (let's say for Gmail), you'll see the "Personal Results" switch on the top-right of Google's search results page.

When Google "Personal Results" is on (Image 2.4), Google will check your social network connections (e.g. Twitter, Google+) and display search results from people to whom you're connected first. In other words, regular Google ranking is ignored until your personal results have been displayed.

Image 2.4: Google "Personal Results" on.

When Google "Personal Results" is off (Image 2.5), Google will display search results solely based on Google ranking.

Image 2.5: Google "Personal Results" off.

When I am doing search engine optimization (SEO) research, whether for my clients or myself, I always turn Google "Personal Results" off. Otherwise, the search results that appear on Google's first page will be driven by my connections, rather than pure search rank (which is what I want to check in this case).

As you can see, content marketing provides a significant long-term return on your marketing dollars, meaning that you'll make more money selling your products and services. And that's a good thing.

> Content marketing can help you make more money and that's a good thing.

> You may find it interesting that many of the posts that drive the most traffic to my site were created using content curation, a content creation tactic where you select links to the best content on a subject and write a short blurb to appear next to each link to provide context.
>
> It's a great way to create useful content quickly and, as you can see in the "1000+ Content Ideas for Your Blog or Newsletter" example above, it's effective. Learn how to use the content curation approach by taking my "Quickly and Easily Create Content For the Web!" course at: http://bit.ly/1eLffCd

Before moving on to the third part of our core goal, let's go over our core goal one more time (promise!). The core goal of content marketing is:

To **drive targeted traffic** to your website **month-after-month** while **building authority, goodwill and trust**.

Building Authority, Goodwill and Trust

Up to now, we've looked at how to use content to drive targeted traffic month-after-month. Now we'll look at the softer, though no less important, side of content marketing: building trust. Trust is one of the keys to selling. Why?

People buy from businesses that they trust.

People don't buy from businesses that they don't trust.

How does content marketing build trust? By building your authority, creating goodwill and enabling social proof.

Building Authority

These days, everyone is an expert.

Or, at least that's what they'd like you to think. With so many self-proclaimed experts online, how can you establish yourself as a real one? With content of course! By posting useful content that helps answer your target customer's questions and solve their problems, you're demonstrating that you know what you're talking about. This isn't showing off – you're honestly trying to help them and that will make visitors to your site feel good and prove that you're the real thing. While this aspect of content marketing benefits all content marketers, it's especially useful to service professionals like lawyers, realtors, coaches and more. That's because service folks are selling expertise. Using content to prove their expertise leads to a better chance that their site visitors will purchase those services.

> The authority that content marketing helps build is especially useful to businesses that sell services such as lawyers, realtors and coaches.

Creating Goodwill

People like to buy from folks that they like. Content marketing is how you lead folks to like you. The key is that you're helping them for free. By posting content that answers their questions and solves their problems, you're a hero! You were there when they needed you and, man, they will come back again and again. Hero worship aside, the warm feelings your content readers have will make them more likely to buy from you and that's one of your most important business goals.

> Never underestimate the power of goodwill.

Enabling Social Proof

The last aspect to using content marketing to build trust is social proof. Social proof demonstrates that folks trust you, and that, in turn, makes more folks trust you.

> Social proof demonstrates that folks trust you, and that, in turn, makes more folks trust you.

Here are some things that provide social proof:

- The size of your online community including Twitter followers, Facebook fans, LinkedIn connections, newsletter subscribers and more.
- Your guest posts because, as mentioned earlier, a guest post is an endorsement of you and your business by the owner of that site.
- The number of comments and social shares your content receives (Image 2.6). How many folks comment on your content? How often

is your content shared on social networks? The higher the numbers, the greater the social proof.

Image 2.6: Here's social proof that people really liked this post.

The Benefits of Content Marketing - Recap

Let me recap the benefits of inbound marketing in Table 2.7:

Who	What	Benefits
Content Marketer	Creates Useful Content and Casts Their Net Online	Website ranks higher in natural search engine results which leads to an increased amount of targeted site traffic and thus more people exposed to your products and services More links to your content on other sites leads to an increased amount of targeted site traffic and thus more people exposed to your products and services Increases the odds of a purchase by building trust through authority, goodwill and social proof

Who	What	Benefits
Search Engine	Indexes Useful Content	Helps searchers find what they are looking for more quickly resulting in a higher number of repeat searchers leading to a greater chance to earn income when ad links are clicked
Customers	Searches for Useful Content	Find answers to their questions and problems quickly and easily when searching Discovers businesses which can demonstrate their knowledge, thus building trust and reassuring them when making a purchase Discovers businesses that offer relevant products and services around their current area of interest

Table 2.7: The benefits of content marketing.

The Real Life Value of Content Marketing – The Proof is Out There

In closing, I'd like to provide you with links that lead to more real life information about the benefits of content marketing. To see real life content marketing case studies and success stories, visit: http://bit.ly/Wdis9V.

Bibliography

[1] "Study Guides and Strategies," accessed February 26, 2013,

http://www.businessbolts.com/content-marketing-survey-report.html

[2] "Study Guides and Strategies," accessed February 26, 2013,

http://www.businessbolts.com/content-marketing-survey-report.html

[3] "Inbound Leads Cost 61% Less Than Outbound [New Data]," accessed February 26, 2013, http://blog.hubspot.com/blog/tabid/6307/bid/31555/Inbound-Leads-Cost-61-Less-Than-Outbound-New-Data.aspx

Chapter 3: Is Content Marketing Right for Your Business?

> **"Nothing is marketed online more than marketing online."**
> *- Matt Mansfield*

One of the **best** things about the web is that there are dozens, if not hundreds, of ways to market your business online. One of the **worst** things about the web is that there are dozens, if not hundreds, of ways to market your business online. So how's a poor small business owner supposed to figure out how they *should* be marketing their business online? That's what this chapter is all about.

Content Marketing and Your Marketing Mix

Every business can benefit at least a little from content marketing and most can benefit a lot. We'll focus on helping you figure out if your business can benefit a little or a lot. Why? Because hype aside, there *are* ways to market your business other than content marketing. Heck, even within content marketing there are different strategies and tactics, some of which will benefit your business more than others. Thus, if you find that the

> Hype aside, there *are* ways to market your business other than content marketing.

potential benefits that your business will receive from using content marketing are little, you may be well served by looking more closely at other approaches.

Most businesses use a variety of marketing strategies and tactics at the same time. Some are online, some are offline, some are outbound, some are inbound, and so on. The group of strategies and tactics that you use across all of your marketing campaigns is called your *marketing mix* and you should figure out where content marketing fits with the rest of your efforts.

To figure out how much of your marketing mix should be devoted to content marketing, you need to evaluate:

1. **How much of an opportunity exists for your business to use content marketing?** Is content marketing the best way to attract your target customers? Will using content marketing for your type of business be a challenge or a walk in the park?

2. **Given the level of opportunity, how much of your marketing mix should you devote to content marketing?** This is important, because most small businesses are in an either/or situation in terms of time and money to spend on marketing. Should you spend your marketing dollars on newspaper advertisements, flyers and magnets? Or, should you spend them on content marketing? You can't do everything so you should focus on the efforts that will give the best results.

Evaluating Content Marketing for Your Business

To determine the level of opportunity that exists for you to use content marketing, reflect on the three questions below with your own business in mind.

This process isn't about whether you should use content marketing or not; as I said earlier, every business can benefit from content marketing. The goal of this chapter is to help you understand how much opportunity exists for content marketing to fit into your marketing mix so you can meet the needs and challenges of your own business.

The good news is that the answers to these questions will help you figure out where content marketing fits best in your marketing mix, a true head start when it's time to select the most effective content marketing strategies and tactics to use for your business.

Ready? Answer the questions below as best you can. By the time you finish the third question, you should have a good idea of how much room there is for content marketing in your marketing mix.

> This process isn't about whether you should use content marketing or not.

Question 1: Is your product or service new or existing?

Whether your marketing mix will lean more towards inbound or outbound tactics has a lot to do with where your offering is in its *life cycle*. Your products and services have a life cycle all their own starting from birth, development and launch, and ending in death, replacement or obsolescence. As you manage your marketing mix, you want to take this life cycle into account. Tactics that are effective during one life cycle stage may not be as effective during another. How does that impact content marketing? In Chapter 1 you learned that outbound marketing tactics try to catch a customer's attention by interrupting what they are currently doing, while content marketing tactics try to catch a customer's attention by assisting them in what they are already doing.

Looking at these two contrasting ideas, the biggest weakness of content marketing is revealed: *you cannot assist someone in what they are already doing if they are not already doing something*. In other words, if your target customers aren't online looking for information about your new products or services, content marketing may not be the most effective approach for your business at this time.

That's not to say that you can't use content marketing when a new product is launched. By using content that emphasizes the benefits of your products and services and resolving the questions and problems of your target customers, there are lots of opportunities for content marketing to play a role. However, when a product or service is new, outbound marketing will likely be the fastest way to get a target customer's attention. Let's use the Apple iPad as an example to see this idea in action.

A Real-Life New Product Content Marketing Success Story

When the iPad was introduced, not many folks were looking for a product like it. Apple had to run flashy ads on TV and in print in order to grab the customer's attention. **The takeaway** is that outbound marketing can bring fast results for products and services that are early in their life cycle.

After the iPad had launched and was known throughout the marketplace, content marketing efforts could be used to good effect as we see in this real-life content marketing success story:

In 2010, a good friend of mine, Shane Ketterman, started a blog at http://www.tcgeeks.com that focused on the Apple iPad. He wrote tons of useful content including hardware reviews, app reviews and roundups and tips and tricks on how to use the iPad.

Shane's content brought droves of search engine and social media users to his site where, in addition to his great content, he also sold iPad accessories and apps through Apple and Amazon affiliate programs. Shane built his traffic up so high that he was able to successfully sell the site in less than one year for a nice sum of money.

The takeaway is that content marketing can become much more effective once a product or service has been entrenched in the marketplace using outbound marketing.

Keep in mind that, even if your business is new, the products and services you offer may already be well established in the marketplace like consulting, accounting, project management software and others. That means that your customers are already online looking for information so content marketing tactics will fit into your marketing mix just fine.

Question 2: Is your industry already saturated with online content?

Competition is a two-edged sword. When your business faces high competition it means that there's high demand for your type of products and services and that there's likely a high supply of content about your type of products and services online already. If there's a high demand for your offering, then you should be OK. I mean, when you chose to go into a particular type of business, you evaluated and OK'd the risks of competition beforehand, right? If the supply of content is high so that you're facing content saturation, that's a more difficult challenge. Breaking through the noise online will take more creativity, effort and time.

At a high-level, you can get an idea if your industry is saturated with online content by using a simple Google search. Let's take the industry keyword phrase, "life coach" for example. When I searched for "life coach" on Google, I got this result:

There are 565,000,000 results – that means there's a lot of online competition for this industry. However, when I search for the industry keyword phrase, "Belly Dancer" on Google, this is what came up:

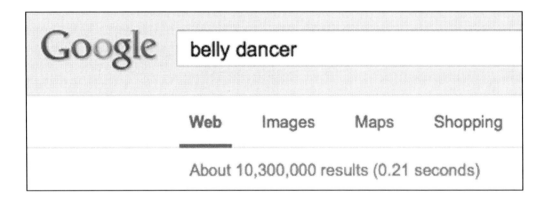

Here, I got 10,300,000 results which tells me that the belly dancing industry is far less competitive online than the life coach industry (who knew?). You may think that 10,300,000 results is still pretty competitive, but since this is the most general keyword phrase for that industry it will have a lot of results; results that can be trimmed down using the topic techniques discussed in chapter 4.

Want an example of a *really* competitive industry? Here are the results when I searched for the industry keyword phrase, "online marketing":

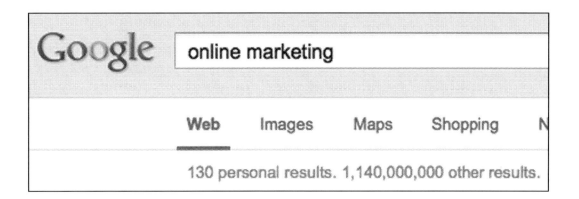

That's 1,140,000,000 results - now that's some hefty competition! It supports my observation: "Nothing is marketed online more than marketing online."

This is a high-level view; it's a method to help you get a gut feel for the level of competition that your content will face online. The good news is that it's perfectly possible to use content marketing in a saturated industry – it just costs more in terms of time and effort, which is something you'll want to take into account when formulating your marketing mix.

Question 3: Is your business local?

If your product or service can be sold over a wide area, national or global, then more traditional content marketing tactics like blogging, videos, and podcasts are a great way to drive targeted traffic to your site. However, if your product or service is one that can only be used locally like landscaping, hair styling, dry cleaning and the like, then you have a different challenge.

For local businesses, customers rarely search for information online beyond looking up which is the closest to them. That's because a lot of these services are selected from referrals – a customer asks a friend which one they like and then the customer gives that business a try.

> The exception to this is online reviews and menus. Potential customers often want to find reviews beyond the referrals and menus are a critical piece of content to have on both your website and posted at dining sites online.

Because of this, standard content marketing tactics such as blogging and videos are less effective for local businesses. Instead, local businesses will have to be more creative when deciding which content marketing tactics to use. Here's a real life content marketing success story that illustrates how the business owners effectively combined the use of online tools with content marketing tactics to successfully engage their customers on a regular basis.

A Real-Life Local Business Content Marketing Success Story

I first met Jolene Loetscher when she served as one of my marketing and Public Relations professionals in the *Matt About Business* post, "5 Successful Marketers Reveal Their Favorite Public Relations Tools."

While interviewing Jolene for that post, we talked about the side business she and her husband Nate run, DooGooders, a pet waste removal company. They're hired to go to people's houses and clean up the pet poop for the owner. The thing that really got my attention was the approach they use to interact and engage with their customers.

Now, you may find the subject matter unpleasant, but the way Jolene and Nate approach their service business is anything but. From cutesy taglines and sayings to helpful and relevant blog content to fun and engaging design, DooGooders hits every marketing note right. The most interesting thing is the tools they use to interact with their customers and, for them, finding the right tools was essential.

Finding the Right Tools was Essential

"This is a low-margin business," says Nate. "Because of that, we need to watch our costs and keep our staff low."

"This fact," adds Jolene, "led us to look for efficient and low-cost ways to run the business."

For the sake of efficiency, and because most of their customers are busy, two-income homes which need quick and easy ways to get things done, almost 100% of DooGooders transactions happen on their site via PayPal.

"Sometimes we don't even meet our customers face-to-face, "says Nate. "We just get a paid order with an address."

Because of the hands-off approach, the couple had the problem of how to update each customer when their yard was serviced.

"We wanted our customer relations to be high-touch and create loyalty," says Jolene. "But, we also had to watch the time and cost of the effort to be so." High-touch customer relations and creating loyalty are both spots where content marketing shines. Nate and Jolene found free solutions to their problem that work well together.

Two Free Solutions That Work Together

The process they devised was simple, powerful and, best of all, free.

When a customer signs up with DooGooders, they're assigned a DooGooders number and given a location on Foursquare, the popular location-based check-in service.

"For the sake of privacy and safety, we don't use the exact customer address," says Nate. "Instead, we use their assigned DooGooders number combined with their street and pet names."

Each time a customer's yard is serviced, the DooGooders field service employee checks-in using Foursquare to mark the job done. In turn, that check-in update is posted to Twitter for the customer to see by either following the DooGooders' Twitter account directly or checking the DooGooders' blog page to see the live Twitter updates there.

"Our customers really love getting this notification, "says Jolene. "Not only do they receive confirmation that the cleanup has been done, it feels very personal as if a special message has been sent just for them and really, that's exactly what it is!"

Two More Business Benefits

Using Foursquare and having the check-in notifications show up on Twitter and on DooGooder's blog page provide two more important business benefits.

"When we post on Foursquare," says Nate, "people are notified about our locations being visited. In a way, this has served as good free advertising for us because folks see our name and check our site out online which has led to sales."

That's casting your net and social proof at work right there!

Another important benefit is extending the high-touch relationship with their customers beyond the notifications.

"We continually write engaging and relevant blog posts which our customers read and comment upon, both on Twitter and on our site," says Jolene. "The notifications keep them coming back to the Twitter feed or the site and the content keeps them engaged with us and helps build community."

DooGooders also sends regular e-mail newsletters to their customers, each of which is chock-full of content and relevant offers. Though neither Nate nor Jolene mentioned it, their customers are regularly are exposed to their Twitter feed and blog site. That means DooGooders can send messages about deals and promotions such as "Refer a friend, get 1 free service visit" and other ideas they come up with.

The Takeaway

The takeaway from the DooGooders' story is that staying in touch with field personnel and building customer relationships is easier and less expensive than ever. All it takes is the right tools and a bit of creativity.

The approach DooGooders devised can be easily duplicated by service companies to reap similar benefits. Landscapers, home cleaning teams and carpet cleaning services are a few that come to mind. The DooGooder's success story is a great example of how to use a combination of tactics to target customers via content and online tools by:

- Engaging customers when and where they would like to be engaged (targeting) via tools such as online notifications that service has been rendered (content);
- Building trust by offering multiple touch-points both online (targeting) and via e-mail (content) as well as an ongoing campaign of engagement via their blog (content, casting your net and social proof); and
- Driving sales though the use of e-mail marketing (content), social sites such as Foursquare and social networks like Twitter (targeting) where they can offer discounts and other promotions.

How Does Content Marketing Fit Into Your Marketing Mix?

You'll get a good feel for how content marketing will fit into your marketing mix by using your answers to the three questions.

If your answers tend towards the *less challenging, more opportunity* side of content marketing with a well-established product or service, low online content competition and specialized non-local products and services, then content marketing may be more effective for you.

However, if your answers tended towards the *more challenging, less opportunity* side of content marketing with a new product or service, high online content competition and local commodity products and services, then content marketing may be less effective for you.

In either case, content marketing will still be effective. As a time-crunched small business owner, you'll want to carefully evaluate each approach before formulating your marketing mix. If you're on the more challenging, less opportunity side of the spectrum, you may want to use fewer content marketing tactics for now and start using more as conditions change throughout your product or service's life cycle. You'll likely end up using a combination of both outbound and inbound tactics to achieve your business goals and that's just fine.

SECTION II: Take Your First Steps Toward Creating Great Content

If you determine that content marketing is a good fit for your business, then the aim of the following two chapters is to lay the foundation for content creation. We'll discuss:

1) What goes into creating great content, and

2) How to get past the most common hurdles to creating content.

Chapter 4: What Makes Great Content?

"What kind of content do I need on my website?"

That's a great question and one that my clients frequently ask. It presents a perfect opportunity for me to sit down and explain the role that great content plays in the success of their website.

There are two types of website content: site content and marketing content.

Site Content

This is the standard stuff that your customers expect to find on your website and includes all this and more:

- The About page;
- The Frequently asked Questions (FAQ) page;
- A Contact Us page or form;
- A Privacy Policy page; and, if needed,
- A Terms of Use page.

Marketing Content

This includes all the articles, blog posts, white papers, e-books, slideshows, videos, images, infographics, podcasts and more on your site. This is the material that's used for content marketing. It will drive targeted traffic to your site month-after-month.

In this chapter, we're going to take a deep dive into the parts that make up each piece

> By the end of this chapter, you'll know the parts that make up each piece of content and how to polish them to make your content shine.

of marketing content. By the end, you'll know how to make each piece of content shine.

The Three Parts of Marketing Content

Every piece of online marketing content is made up of three parts:

1. **The Topic -** what the content is about;
2. **The Information-** the content's actual text, images, videos, audio, etc.; and
3. **The Design -** how the content is presented.

These parts need to work together to create an effective piece of content. If even one part is off, your content marketing efforts won't go far. However, here's one word (well, it's really an acronym) that makes all three work harder and be more effective: WIFM.

> The three parts of content need to work together to be effective.

What's In It For Me (WIFM)

> Your target customers aren't thinking about your business or your products and services. They're online to get something done.

Your target customers are online to get something done. The goal of content marketing is to help them find the information they want and need. When they come to your site to get that information you have the opportunity to expose them to your product and service offerings. While searching online, your customers are thinking about their problems and needs. They're not thinking about your business or your products and services. They're in full on "What's in it For Me mode!" That's why WIFM is so important to consider when you create content.

Your marketing content should help your customers answer their questions and solve their problems. It shouldn't be sales-ey and may not even mention your products or services very often. That's because another goal of content marketing is to build trust and no one likes to be lured in with a promise that's not fulfilled. However, that's exactly what you're doing if you create content that seems to have the information a customer needs but in reality is either full of useless, generic information or presents a hard-sell pitch.

> Your marketing content should help your customers answer their questions and solve their problems

I'll talk about WIFM more as we take a closer look at each of the three parts of great content. Keeping your target customer's needs and problems in mind is the key to creating great content.

> Keeping your target customer's needs and problems in mind is the key to creating great content.

The Topic

The topic is essentially what a piece of content is about (Image 4.1). For example, the topic of this section is explaining the topic part of content.

Topics can range far and wide depending on a number of factors:

- Your business type -business to consumer (B2C) or business to business (B2B);

- The types of products and services you offer - for example, do your products need post-sales support? and

- The information your target customers search for online.

Image 4.1: The topic should be established using the contents title. Source: http://bit.ly/1jIcHZQ

Different types of businesses might have topics ranging from how to choose the best car for a family of six to how healthy someone should be to start working out or how to use direct deposit to dramatically lower payroll costs. These are all topics that consumers and businesses search for online. However, to discover what *your* target customers are looking for online, you need to get inside their heads. The key to doing that is research.

> To discover what *your* target customers are looking for online, you need to get inside their heads.

Researching Topics for Your Content

There are two ways to research topics that interest your target customers. One is to just ask them straight out via your blog, an e-mail newsletter, an online survey or on social networks. The other way is to study historical data from search engines and social media networks.

Researching Topics: Ask Your Target Customer

Directly asking your target customers about what topics they would like to know more about is useful in learning more about the information they would like to find online. These days, you can conduct this kind of research without having people physically present as with focus groups, and many of the methods for asking directly are inexpensive, easy-to-use and effective.

When using this approach, keep in mind that there are two downsides to asking folks directly about what they want. First, people aren't always honest when they're asked directly about their wants and needs. Either they're uncomfortable talking about personal things with

> There are two downsides to asking folks directly about what they want.

a stranger or they don't want to look stupid in front of someone else because they may not have the answers to basic questions. In either case, the answers you get from asking straight out might not be the most accurate representation of the topics people are truly looking for.

Second, getting folks to take the time to respond to you is always difficult. People are busy and the amount of information you receive by asking about topics directly will be less than you can gather by studying historical data. One way around this low response rate is to offer an incentive such as a chance to win an iPad in exchange for answering the question. However, this approach can get costly in the long run.

These two points aside, here are three methods you can use to ask direct questions.

Ask Your Target Customers: Online Surveys

Forget about walking around the mall with a clipboard - online surveys allow you to post a series of questions and begin receiving replies immediately. A couple of survey solutions I like:

> **Qualaroo** (www.qualaroo.com) - Essentially, this solution pops up a survey for each of your site visitors to take. It's not nearly as annoying as it sounds and I've seen great results using it on my small business blog site, www.mattaboutbusiness.com. You can start using Qualaroo for free and get great results but the premium options include more entries, additional surveys, white-label branding and more. Take a look at Image 4.2 to see what a Qualaroo survey looks like on my site.

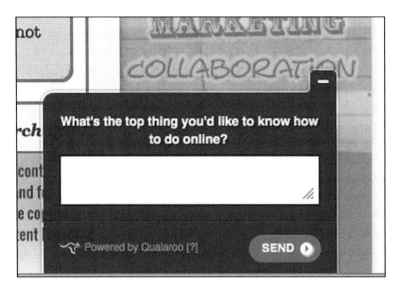

Image 4.2: This is what a Qualaroo survey looks like when it pops-up at the bottom of my www.mattaboutbusiness.com site.

Wufoo (www.wufoo.com) - For a more complex survey, Wufoo is my go-to solution. Using Wufoo, you can create single or multi-page surveys with built-in logic that directs them to do "this" if they answer "that", the ability to change the entire look and feel to match your business' branding, the capability to embed the survey directly into your site and many more bells and whistles. Like Qualaroo, you can start using Wufoo for free, but the premium plans are affordable and worth considering.

Ask Your Target Customers: Social Media

Thanks to social media networks such as Twitter, Facebook and LinkedIn, asking your target customers about their needs and problems is as easy as 1-2-3. Aside from asking questions, Facebook (Image 4.3) offers the ability to create polls for free, another great way to tap into your markets directly. Lastly, because most of the folks who see your stuff on social media have already chosen to pay attention to you, the response rate will likely be higher than a survey.

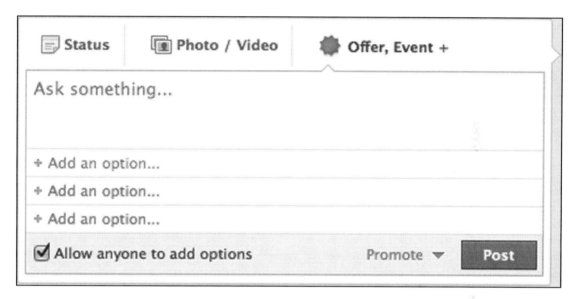

Image 4.3: You can add a question and then add poll options
by clicking the "Offer, Event +" option on your Facebook page.

Ask Your Target Customers: E-Mail Newsletters

E-mail newsletters are another great vehicle for asking your target customers about their problems and needs. For example you can use them to ask folks to reply to your e-mail to answer a question you ask or include a link to an online survey built with Wufoo.

Since your e-mail subscribers have chosen to pay attention to you the response rate will likely be higher than asking questions with surveys and social media. It's easy to follow or become a fan of someone on social media. Your e-mail subscribers had to fill in a form and then click on a link in an e-mail to confirm their subscription. Simply put: they have invested more time and effort in you and your content.

Derek Halpern, the online marketing strategist over at http://www.socialtriggers.com, shares one of the key contributions to his blog reader's high loyalty, customer satisfaction and conversion rates. That key is to start a conversation that begins a relationship as early as possible. How does he get a conversation started? When someone signs up for his newsletter, he sends back an e-mail with two things:

- A thank you, and
- A simple question: "What are you struggling with?"

That question opens the door for his subscribers to tell him directly exactly what they need and is a great way to get his target customer more engaged in the products and services he has to offer or recommend.

Researching Topics: Study Historical Data

As you read this, your target customers are online searching for and discussing the information they need to solve their problems. Each time a search is run on a search engine or a discussion is held on a social media network, a record is added to the database of the system they're using such as Google, Facebook, and others. Thankfully, and critically for content marketing, most of these systems allow you to run reports on those records.

Unlike asking straight out, the answers from these reports are refreshingly honest. They're based on real actions that have already taken place. Using the information in these reports, you can discover the single keywords or keyword phrases related to your product and service offerings that are searched for and discussed the most often.

For each keyword you can see the demand for the keyword in the number of searches plus the number of discussions on social networks. You can also gauge the

> **Definition:** a keyword is the word or phrase that your customers actually use to search for, and discuss, their problems and needs online.
>
> Discovering the actual keywords used by your target market is a crucial ingredient for content marketing success. Find out more about keywords in my recorded webinar "SEO in Everyday English" at:
>
> http://bit.ly/1cHUrdO.

supply of information by learning how many of your competitors already offer content on, or bid on paid advertising for, that topic.

I love this approach! Instead of trying to guess the keywords that your target customers use, you'll have the actual words and phrases that they're interested in. That's the best part of this method, and makes all the difference in the effectiveness of your content marketing.

With these keywords in hand, you can identify the topics with the highest demand and the lowest supply (the juicy topics) and use them to create content that will drive ridiculous amounts of traffic to your website. Discovering juicy keywords is one of the keys to driving targeted traffic to your website

> Discovering juicy keywords is one of the keys to driving targeted traffic to your website.

because they address the topic most likely to land you on the front page of Google's search results.

Let's take a look at how to use search engine and social media research to find great topic ideas for your content.

Study Historical Data: Using Search History

Search engine history is a goldmine of keyword information. For each search made, a record is kept of the word or phrase used in the search. Add them all up and you get the online demand for information about specific topics. There are a lot (and I mean a *lot*) of ways to get at this search information. We're going to take a look at two of them in this section. First we'll use Google's Keyword Planner to run reports on the searches made at Google. Then, we'll use Google Analytics to run reports on searches that actually led visitors to your site.

> Search engine history is a goldmine of keyword information.

Why Only Google?

Before we move on, let me address the reason why Google is the only search engine we'll research, but, honestly, there's not much to discuss. It's a matter of efficiency. As you can see in Image 4.4, Google has the highest search market share by far.

These numbers say that 67% of all searches made in the US in January, 2013 were made with Google. Given that, Google has a large enough database for us to use to uncover oodles of juicy topics. Let's face it: I'm not a data analyst and likely, neither are you. We have content to create and a business to run. Using Google as the standard allows us to find topics that do well on all search engines.

comScore Explicit Core Search Share Report* January 2013 vs. December 2012 Total U.S. – Home & Work Locations Source: comScore qSearch			
Core Search Entity	**Explicit Core Search Share (%)**		
	Dec-12	Jan-13	Point Change
Total Explicit Core Search	*100.0%*	*100.0%*	*N/A*
Google Sites	66.7%	67.0%	0.3
Microsoft Sites	16.3%	16.5%	0.2
Yahoo! Sites	12.2%	12.1%	-0.1
Ask Network	3.0%	2.8%	-0.2
AOL, Inc.	1.8%	1.7%	-0.1

Image 4.4: The percentage of the search market owned by different search engines. [1]

Using Search History: Google's Keyword Planner

The Keyword Planner is part of the Google AdWords toolset so you'll need to create both a Google account and an AdWords account to use it. The good news is that both types of accounts are free as is the use of the Keyword Planner (which I'll call "the KP" from here on).

The only drawback to the KP is that it's less functional and accurate than for-pay tools such as Market Samurai and Wordtracker. This shouldn't stop you from using the tool - it's still a great way to find juicy content topics.

> **Keyword Tool vs. Keyword Planner**
>
> If you're wondering why I'm not using Google's Keyword Tool, it's because the new Google Keyword Planner replaced it in 2013. If you're familiar with the older tool, you might want to head on over to http://bit.ly/1fZ87bu to learn more about the differences between the two solutions before continuing (there's a great chart highlighting the differences between the two solutions toward the bottom of the post). If you're not familiar with the older tool, just ignore this box and move on.

In the remainder of this section, I'll walk you through the most basic yet powerful way to use the KP for discovering content topic ideas. Yep, there's more than one-way to make use of the feature-rich KP, many of which you may want to explore after you get your feet wet below.

To learn more about those features, you can visit http://bit.ly/1dXXIXu or search for *"using keyword planner"* over at Google to find step-by-step guides like the one I've created here.

Ready to discover some great topics? Let's go!

Create Your "Seed" List

Before you hop online, spend some time creating a list of the broadest, most high-level words and phrases that your target customers would use when searching for information about your type of products and services. This is called a "seed list" as the Keyword planner will use each of these "seeds" to grow a list of new and valuable keywords and keyword phrases. A couple of points to keep in mind:

1. If you've spent any time optimizing your site for search, you may already have created a list like this. If so, it's fine to go ahead and use that one for this exercise.

2. Throughout this walkthrough, we're going to pretend we're a life coach (or not pretend if you *are* a life coach) so I'll start with the keyword phrase, "life coach."

Login to Google Adwords and Open the Keyword Planner

Now it's time to get online and head over to the Keyword Planner. If you're not already logged into your Google account, login at: http://bit.ly/1bzjvBO.

> **Need to create a Google account?**
> Head over to: http://bit.ly/1ndaj1S to create one (tip: if you use Gmail, you already have a Google account.)

If you already have an Adwords account, then head on over to Adwords at: http://bit.ly/N1gxRv.

> **Need to create an Adwords account?**
> Get one at http://bit.ly/1qpMTFA by clicking the "Get started now." button.

Once you're logged into Adwords, navigate to the Keyword Planner as shown in Image 4.5.

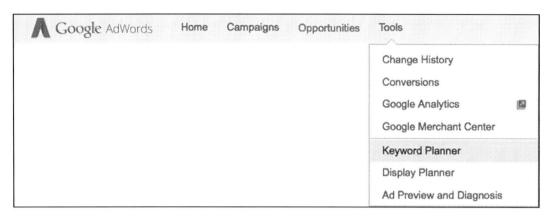

*Image 4.5: Head on over to the Keyword Planner
using the link under the "Tools" menu.*

As shown in Image 4.6, click on the first option in the KP, "Search for new keyword and ad group ideas". This will open the search form shown in Image 4.7.

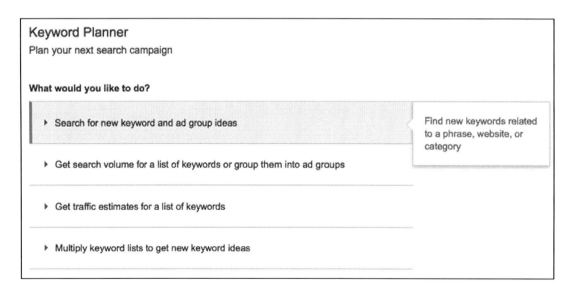

Image 4.6: Select the first option, "Search for new keywords and ad group ideas."

The Keyword Planner Search Form

As you can see in Image 4.7, this form has a lot of settings to play with however, let's start with the configuration I use most when looking for topics.

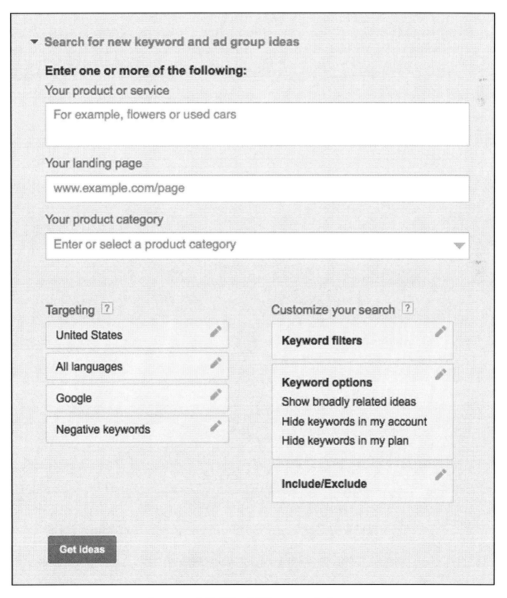

Image 4.7: The KP's search form.

Start by entering the keywords and keyword phrases from the seed list you created earlier into the "Your product or service" box. Each entry should be either on a new line or separated by a comma.

I like to set "Only show ideas closely related to my search terms" so that my search results are relevant. To do so, click on the pencil to the right of "Keyword options" (Image 4.7) and click on the toggle switch to apply the filter (Image 4.8).

When I want to get lots of ideas, I unclick this option to get some wild, but sometimes usable, keyword results.

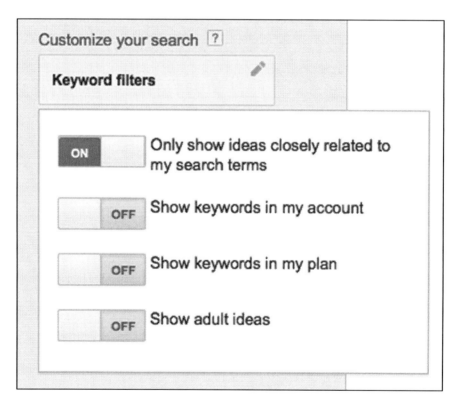

Image 4.8: Toggle on the "Only show ideas closely related to my search terms" option.

Next, click the "Get Ideas" button. Exciting isn't it?

The Keyword Planner Search Results Screen

After Google spins its wheels for a bit, the results of your search will be shown. You can see the results from our "life coach" search in Image 4.9. To make the image more readable, I've broken it down into two separate parts for a closer look. First we'll look at what's in the search results on the right (A) and then I'll give you an overview of the super-handy options available on the left (B). Lastly we'll discuss how to use both the right and left side to discover juicy topics for your content (A + B=C).

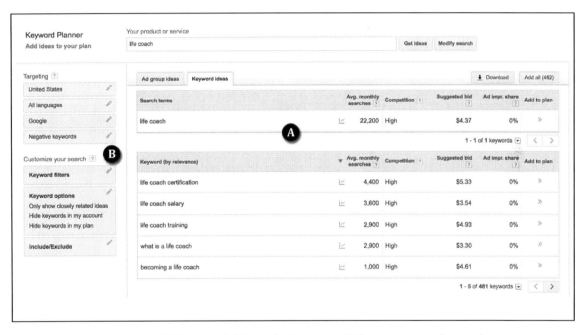

Image 4.9: "life coach" Google Keyword Planner search results.

(A) Keyword Planner: Your Search Results

Within the search results that Google returned are the topic ideas we're looking for. Using Image 4.10, I'll explain each part of the search results section and how to use the results of the search to discover topics for your content.

Image 4.10: The search results returned by Google. There are topic ideas in here!

(a) Click on the "Keyword ideas" tab

Since you're looking for keywords (i.e. topic ideas), you should make sure you're actually looking at the search results you need. The "Ad group ideas" tab is there if you want to use paid advertising to drive targeted traffic. Nothing wrong with that; it's just not what we're doing right now.

(b) Saving Your Search Results Offline

You can work with your search results here or export them to a spreadsheet and dig in offline. Both have their ups and downs, but to really get the best results out of this process, staying online is the way to go. That's because you can use all the handy filtering tools that Google provides up to and including running a new search directly from the search results page. I typically use the download feature when I want a snapshot in time or if I want to create and share a list of the results without having to cut and paste or retype anything.

(c) Results for Exact Keywords

This top section will display the results for the exact keywords and keyword phrases you entered from your seed list, in this case, "life coach." I'll explain the columns further in (d), (e), (f) and (g) below.

A few notes before we move on:

- The search results will always be specific to the targeting and filtering rules of your search. This was one of the nifty features I glossed over earlier but no worries, you can just accept the default at that time and then adjust the targeting using the options in the left sidebar.
- To sort by a particular column, simply click the column title. Clicking it again will result in a reverse sort.
- Hovering your mouse cursor over the "?" next to a column's name will pop-up a box with information about that column.

(d) Keyword (i.e. Topic Ideas)

These are the words or phrases that people actually search for on Google. Each one is included within your search results based on Google's algorithm which is the super-sophisticated formula they've created to build relationships between search terms that match the real world.

Since we used the "Only show ideas closely related to my search terms" filter, we are presented with a list that's fairly relevant to our search term of "life coach" and that significantly cuts down the number of rows we need to review to find juicy topics.

(e) Avg. Monthly Searches

This column displays the number of times a specific word or phrase was searched for, on a 12-month average, each month. This is key because now you know how many people are looking for specific information via Google search which is the demand. A high demand means that many folks are interested in that topic. In content marketing terms that translates into *creating content to serve that demand can drive targeted traffic to my site so I'll add that topic to my list of content to be created.*

A low demand isn't necessarily a bad thing. Even if only five hundred people search for a topic monthly, *that's five hundred target customers* who can find your content while searching and then visit your site. With some content marketing experience under your belt, you'll find that some low demand keywords drive enough traffic to justify the cost of creating content while others don't. To start, a rule of thumb is that 100 searches or less per month is too low.

(f) Competition

If the "Avg. Monthly Searches" column is demand, then the "Competition" column is supply. The three levels used in this column, "High", Medium" and "Low", provide an indication of how many businesses are *bidding* on a specific word or phrase (i.e. paid search ads). These businesses are likely targeting the same customers are you and, if they are also using content marketing tactics, they are your competitors in the search results.

The competition number means something different when you use a for-pay tool such as Market Samurai and Wordtracker. There, the number tells you the actual level of existing content supply for each keyword. A high number means that a lot of other businesses have already created content on their websites for a specific word or phrase, something that's much more useful to know than how many folks are bidding on it for advertising. The KP's competition ranking is a decent indicator however, and it's free.

(g) Adwords Stuff

The three (g) sections in Image 4.10 are used specifically for Adwords. For the most part, you can ignore them unless you're interested in paid advertising.

(h) Page and View Controls

Clicking on the down arrow here allows you to set how many keywords are displayed at one time up to 100. The arrows are used to navigate between results pages.

(i) Search

The form at the top of the page enables you to search for either a specific term or comma separated terms using the same settings as before by clicking on the "Get ideas" button. You can also change up your options a bit using the "Modify search" button. It's a handy way to search for something else without having to go all the way back to the main form.

(B) Keyword Planner: Targeting and Filtering Your Search Results

As shown in Image 4.11, the left sidebar contains many options that enable you to refine your search. Any of the options can be changed by clicking on the pencil in the top right of each option set. Playing with these options can turn up good topic ideas, so take some time to explore what each one does.

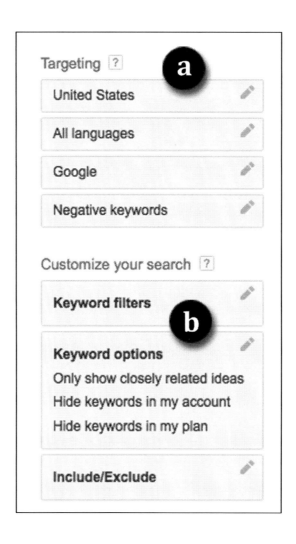

Image 4.11: The options available for refining your search.

(a) Targeting

Use options such as geography and language to hone in on your target customers where they live.

(b) Customize Your Search

Here, you can tighten your focus even further by filtering your search results in many ways.

(C) Keyword Planner: Using the Search Results to Discover Juicy Topic Ideas

Now that we have our search results and have targeted and filtered them to our satisfaction, it's time to start digging for juicy topic ideas. The goal here is to find keywords with high demand as measured by the "Avg. monthly searches" column and medium or low supply as measured by the "Competition" column.

> You can certainly use topics with both high demand and high supply; in fact I recommend doing so. You may never appear on the front page of Google with those topics, but it will serve to round out your site with content that your customers expect to be there and that will increase the time they spend on your site.
>
> However, if driving traffic is your primary goal, then juicy topics are the way to go!

After digging into the search results for "life coach", I discovered keywords for three main topic themes.

- ***What is a life coach?*** – This is a great topic for a life coach site and it can be used to differentiate the specific approach used by this life coach vs. other coaches.

- ***How do I find a life coach?*** – Another great topic and one that can lead to many different pieces of content. A life coach could create a video, a checklist, a blog post, an infographic and more, each addressing the topic of finding and selecting a life coach.

- ***How do I become a life coach?*** – This one may not appear relevant, as most life coaches want folks to hire them as a life coach as opposed to having their customers becoming life coaches themselves! Read on however:

  - **Real-life story:** when I dug into this keyword further, I came across one keyword phrase, "how much should I charge as a life coach". A client of mine who is a life coach used this topic to create a blog post that discussed ways to tell if your life coach was charging the right amount. That post drove more traffic to his site than any other.

As we look further into the results, we can find additional keywords to use for even more content topics.

- ***Certification for life coach*** – Another topic that seems as if it's only for life coaches that could be turned on its head and used to create content on the different types of certifications and whether or not the certification matters to the client when choosing a life coach.

- ***Life coaching on line*** – Can you hire an online life coach? How effective is that option? What are the pros and cons?

- *Life career coaching* – How can a life coach help you with your career? Is that a specialty or something that all life coaches do?
- *Life coaching services* – Another good opportunity to discuss what you offer and perhaps how you partner with other coaches to offer a broader range of services.

I could go on, but you have the idea. Find a high-demand keyword and brainstorm content topics related to that keyword.

Once you've exhausted the possible keywords on your first report, you can run additional reports to find even more topics. Those words and phrases can be more specific than you originally found as well as ones you turned up in your other searches.

More Specific

For example, before I ran more reports for my life coaching client, I asked him to provide me with a list of words and phrases that described what he did. One of them was "set goals" and a search for that phrase on the Google Keyword Tool yielded so many topics that he's still working through them to create content today.

From Other Searches

Sometimes searching for keywords using the words and phrases you identified in other searches can point you toward additional content to create around that topic. To do so, first review your initial search results for prospective topics. Then, using those newly identified topics as a seed list, run more searches to see if any additional keywords can be found.

Using Search History: Google Analytics

Google Analytics is another free tool from Google that tracks the activity on your website including where visitors came from, what they looked at on your site and how long they looked. As you guessed, tracking the activity on your site is crucial for measuring the effects of your content marketing efforts.

But, when it comes to discovering great content topics there's one report from Analytics that can help. That's the "Traffic Sources -> Search -> Organic" report. This handy little report tells you the exact keywords that visitors used to get to your site. It's a historical report that tells you the specific keywords that drove traffic to your site. So, why is that important? By looking at the keywords that led folks to your site, you can discover the actual topics that most interest your target customers and then create even more content around that topic. This approach is a cornerstone of content marketing.

A Real-Life Example from My www.mattaboutbusiness.com Site

While looking at the "Traffic Sources -> Search -> Organic" report one day (Image 4.12), I noticed that a decent amount of traffic came from folks searching for ways to sell online. I had written a post or two on that subject, but nothing extensive. Based on this, I created an e-book called, "Get Started Selling Your Products Online" (check it out at: http://bit.ly/15KdqSD) and started selling it on the site.

So far, sales of the e-book have been brisk and there's even more traffic to my site thanks to the sales page using those keywords. Next, I plan to create more content around selling online, some free and some paid. Each one will drive traffic, establish my expertise, build trust and, ultimately, lead to more business.

Image 4.12: The Google Analytics "Traffic Sources -> Search -> Organic"
report for my Matt About Business site for the keyword "sell."

Study Historical Data: Using Social Media

While using social media to discover content topics is much less accurate than using search (more like finding a needle in a haystack), it's worth mentioning because it's another way to get inside the mind of your target customers.

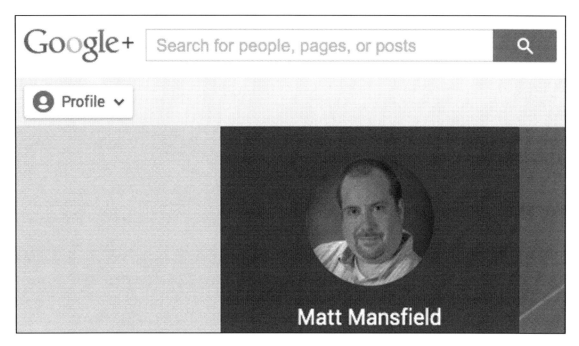

Image 4.13: You can use the bar at the top of any Google+ page

(such as my profile page shown here) to search for keywords and phrases.

The social network with the most accurate search results is Google+. That's because it's part of Google and search is, after all, what they do best. To search for discussions related to your business, simply enter the words and phrases you want to search into the bar at the top of any Google+ page (Image 4.13). If you want to narrow your search, enclose your search term in quotes.

Twitter is another good place to search. Just head over to Twitter search at https://twitter.com/search and enter the words and phrases you want to search. I highly recommend using their advanced search for more useful results by clicking on the "advanced search" link beneath the search box.

Spending some time with the search results from both Google+ and Twitter will not only yield content topic ideas, it'll also help you understand how your target audience talks about your type of offerings; it may even turn up more leads for you to pursue. *Spending time* is the key here. You need to sort through a lot of junk to find the gems, but they're out there waiting for you.

The "Link Bait" Factor

A popular term among online marketers, *link bait* refers to an especially attractive piece of content that other sites want to link to, or even embed on their own site, and that visitors love to share via social media, e-mail and beyond. In a way, all content can be considered link bait but certain high-traffic content types such as infographics and videos provide much juicier bait than others.

What really differentiates a piece of link bait content however is that it doesn't need to adhere to the WIFM rules covered earlier. You see, while link bait content can certainly excel at providing the information your target customers need to answer their questions and solve their problems, it also excels as eye-candy that provides entertainment and, most importantly, drives targeted traffic to your website.

Let's take a closer look at both the positives and negatives of publishing link bait content. Then, I'll discuss a real world example of link bait that netted a lot of fish, ehm, customers.

Link Bait – The Upside

Creating link bait content provides four primary benefits.

Link Bait Benefits – Extended Marketing Reach to Target Customers

When another site mentions your business and links to your site, it greatly extends the reach of your marketing efforts. Even better, sites that link to your content are likely related in some way to your business so there's a good chance that their visitors include your target customers thus your content will be seen by the people who are most likely to buy your products and services.

Link Bait Benefits – Social Proof Leads to Trust

When another site links to content on your site, it's often perceived as an inferred stamp of approval that provides the social proof you need to build the trust that leads to sales.

Link Bait Benefits – Search Engine Optimization Boost

Inbound links from other sites can also increase your own site's search engine ranking, causing it to appear higher on search results pages. When it comes to the site linking in, the higher its rank and the closer its content is to your own in subject matter, the better.

Link Bait Benefits – Sharing is a Good Thing

Link bait content such as an infographic is highly sharable and people love to send a link to the image or even the image itself to their friends, family, business associates, etc. Doing so provides your business with a double whammy:

1. Sharing your content results in an inferred approval of your business by the one sharing which is social proof, and

2. Sharing can lead to a potentially explosive increase in the reach of your marketing efforts as the receiver of shared content may share it with others who also share it and so on.

Link Bait – The Downside

Link bait has its ugly side and, if used improperly, it can do much more harm than good. Here are two examples of link bait gone bad:

1) The act of creating high-traffic driving content using a current event or hot topic is often called "newsjacking". While newsjacking isn't inherently bad, it's a two-edged sword. If you provide useful information related to the event or topic but spin it to help or be relevant to your target customers, you're in the clear. However, if you don't provide useful information and are just using the keywords related to the event or topic to pull in traffic via search, that's a big no-no.

2) If you include a link to a post on a popular blogger's site within one of your own posts, a notice will appear under the linked-to post on their site that includes a link back to the post on your own site. Commonly called a "trackback", this is just fine if the link you include in your post leads to relevant information that adds to your own content. However, if you include the link just to place a trackback on their site to gain a link from a popular site to yours which boosts your search rank and may imply endorsement by the popular blogger, then you've given in to the dark side of link bait.

Link Bait – A Real World Example

A great example of link bait is the infographic shown in Image 4.14. This infographic about media personalities uses the question, "Which are you?" to trigger one of the most riveting types of bait known to humankind: potential humiliation. Every person wants to read through this infographic because they either:

- Fear that they're a "bad personality type", something that could potentially cause humiliation, or
- Believe that they are a "good personality type" and want to validate that viewpoint.

Don't you want to follow the link under the picture to see which personality is closest to yours? My curiosity was the very thing that drew me to the infographic in the first place. Yep, I admit it; the link bait hooked me.

What's interesting about this infographic is that it doesn't even come close to relating to the core business of the creator. The data was gathered, and the analysis of the social media personality types was done, as part of an internal initiative at the company. As Rebecca Dye, social media manager at first direct, explains:

"A lot of people admit to behaving very differently in social media to how they behave in the 'real world' and it's important we're aware of that when we're dealing with customers through a variety of channels. The increased understanding of how people use the likes of Facebook and Twitter will help first direct develop new online customer service initiatives."[4]

The key factor here is that that first direct's business is banking, a subject that holds interest for a wide range of both individuals and businesses. By using the results of the work they did for their own benefit to create an infographic for the public, they were able to throw a very compelling piece of content out on the internet; one that was the perfect link bait. Why? Because social media is a hot topic and, as such, it was likely that other sites would link to the infographic and, as you can see if you search for "a new breed of social media personality" on Google, many, many sites did just that.

This infographic turned link bait into a feeding frenzy and that was a good thing for first direct.

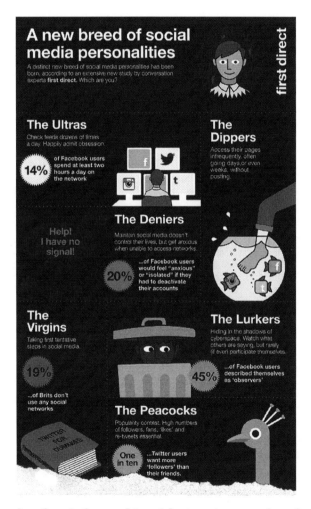

Image 4.14: An example of an infographic with a topic not related to the business' areas of expertise (image credit: A new breed of Social Media Personalities by first direct, on Flickr (http://www.flickr.com/photos/firstdirect/8641833741)).

Never Break Your Topic's Promise

Before we move on to the second part of content, the information, I want to leave you with one important thought: Each and every one of your content topics is a promise that you make to your target customers.

> Each and every one of your content topics is a promise that you make to your target customers.

Why is that? When your target customers are searching for information online, they'll come across your content in their search results. They'll get excited about finding a source of information that will help them fulfill their needs and solve their problems. At that moment, you have made a promise: click on this search result to go to my site and learn what you need to know. Upholding that promise is the role of the information part of your content.

The Information

The basic message of your content is the information (Image 4.15). No matter how your content's information is conveyed, whether by text, audio, video, or some other medium, it should fulfill the promise made by the topic. Why is that so critical? **You need to build trust.**

Why is one of the main goals of content marketing to build trust? Because *people buy from businesses they trust.* Conversely, if they don't trust a business, they're not likely to buy from it. One of the best ways to earn trust is to keep a promise. One of the best ways to lose trust is to break promises.

Are You Blogging Too Often?

by matt mansfield · 5 comments

Share · Tweet 24 · Like 5 · +1 14 · Share 15 · BizSugar 34

One of the most often asked questions about blogging is how often to blog.

Unfortunately, it's also the most often answered questions, too (if you search "how often to blog" on Google you get 1,590,000,000 results!) and therein lies the problem – whose advice do you follow?

The Information

Even cold hard facts don't help here. While it's true that the more content you publish, the more traffic you'll get *(source)*, it's also true that companies that publish new blog posts just 1-2 times per month generate 70% more leads than companies that don't blog at all *(source)*.

None of the advice you find online is necessarily wrong, it's just the right answer for someone else's business.

> None of the advice you find online is necessarily wrong, it's just the right answer for someone else's business.

Image 4.15: The information is the text and images

in this post. Source: http://bit.ly/1jIcHZQ

If the content your visitors find when they get to your site doesn't fulfill the promise of the topic, if it's too generic and high-level or doesn't help them with their needs and problems, they'll turn around and leave and probably not be back. Unfortunately, a lot of potentially great content falls short in information. That happens when the content creator spends time researching topics that interest their target customers, slaps together some high-level information with minimal support and then spends time and effort creating a nice design in text, images, video or audio.

The result? Awesome looking website content that seems interesting at first glance, but falls short in helping website visitors accomplish their goals. Does that kind of content build trust? No siree, it does not. It's just dressing a pig up in lipstick.

The Information: Avoid These Content Pitfalls

Where does poor content information fall short? Here are some of the missing ingredients that can turn great content information into poor content information.

It's Not Actionable

The greatest fault of poor information is non-actionable information that doesn't tell you how to put what you've learned to use. Non-actionable content is hard to use and will fail to be helpful. For example, a blog post that espouses the benefits of using Facebook to extend the reach of your content and engage customers without detailing any of the steps you need to take to use Facebook to achieve those goals.

It's Not Specific Enough or It's Too Specific

Going hand-in-hand with being actionable, if the information is not at the right level of detail for the target audience, it won't be helpful. For example, if the target audience is folks who already know lots about Facebook, then telling them how to create a fan page is too basic for them to find useful. However, if the target audience is people who are Facebook newbies, then explaining why, and how, to build a fan page is right on target.

It's Not Credible

If your content is full of unsupported information, then it will fail to build the trust you need to sell your products and services. All factual claims need to be backed up by supporting evidence, even if it's just a link to the source where you found the information.

It's Not Human-Friendly

All too often, content creators create content to fit search engine optimization (SEO) criteria. Their content is aimed at search engines, not humans. This leads to forced and awkward content that isn't as clear and useful as it could be. Search engines, especially Google, continually strive to make their software as human as possible. In other words, they want their software to evaluate content the same way people do. Therefore, if you write clearly and usefully for humans, the search engines should reward you with higher marks as well.

It's Missing the WIFM

If the information is missing the WIFM (What's In It For Me?) then why should your visitors care about what it tells them? I've seen tons of content that talks about features and functionality but leaves out benefits. For example, don't write a post that tells me all about what your great project management software can do, and how. Instead, write a post that tells me how your great project management software is going to save me time and money (two of my needs for sure!) Use cases and interviews are great tools for adding the WIFM factor. They tell real-life stories of how your products and services have fulfilled the needs and solved the problems of your customers.

It's Too Sales-ey

Nothing turns a prospective customer off more than content that's written to sell. It's even worse if it's a hard, in-your-face sell. While certain content types like white papers and brochures are geared more towards selling, don't worry about making the sale with most of your content. Remember that the goal of content marketing is to drive targeted traffic to your site where visitors will be exposed to your products, services and sales messages as you build credibility and trust.

Feeling a little overwhelmed with all these ingredients? Just remember that content with great information helps your target customers fulfill their needs and solve their problems. If you keep that in mind when creating your content, you'll do just fine.

Real-Life Information Success Story: Strong Content Leads to Successful Viral Marketing

When Joe Chernov joined Eloqua, an online marketing automation vendor, traditional public relations tactics held center stage. "We were telling essentially the same story to the same people over and over," said Chernov. "We weren't reaching out directly to our target markets in order to bring in new interest and leads."

Recognizing that change was needed, Chernov took on a new role, "Director of Content" and began to focus almost entirely on the social web. In this position, he was responsible for identifying, creating and distributing the content that the company should to create in order to bring traffic to their website.

Chernov explains, "We wanted to reach our target audiences where they live on the social web. To accomplish this, we worked hard to create content which is interesting to our target audiences and then distribute that content using social media tools. Using this approach, we've had a lot of success driving targeted traffic to our site." Chernov's increasing use of social media tools led to one of Eloqua's most successful viral marketing campaigns. Aiming to reach Eloqua's main target audience of marketers, Chernov and his team decided to focus on the hot topic of how to use social media tools successfully.

The result was the *Eloqua Social Media Playbook* (http://bit.ly/WkZQCw), a forty-two page e-book that was created as a how to guide for Eloqua's staff to follow on the social web. The guide was billed as "everything Eloqua knows about social media, distilled into one awesomely designed document." It was compiled by Chernov and his team, polished by a creative agency and then posted on the Eloqua blog where anyone could download it for free.

And when Chernov says free, he means free. There's no form to fill out; no form to collect an e-mail address. "We believed that there should be no barriers to getting the guide," says Chernov. "One of our advisory board members, David Meerman Scott, had instilled a company-wide belief that forms kill the spread of content, and we took that to heart."

The results of the "Steal Eloqua's Social Media Playbook" viral marketing campaign exceeded expectations. Viewed over 6,920 times between June 17, 2010 and October 25, 2010, the guide helped establish Eloqua as a leader in online marketing while also driving substantial targeted traffic to their site. Best of all, the campaign keeps running with minimal effort required from Eloqua. Now that's some awesome ROI!

The Design

The design part of your content (Image 4.16) can take it from great to spectacular by making it more engaging and effective.

Image 4.16: This callout box is an example of using design to make the information easier to absorb and understand. Source: http://bit.ly/1jIcHZQ

Like your content's information, your content's design also fulfills the promise made by its topic. Good design makes the information easier to absorb and understand. Design can even make dry information

Good design can make even dry information easier to absorb.

interesting - look at the success of infographics.

I'm not going to talk much in this section about the planning, layout and design of content because that would fill a second book. Each type of content, from text to images, videos, infographics and more, has its own best practices and guidelines. That said, to give you a taste of what good design can do for your content, I'm going to show you some real-world examples of how design can go beyond the look-and-feel of your content to create a brand that's attractive to your target customers.

If you'd like to dive deeper into how to design different types of content, I've already created online courses and eBooks for some and I'm busily creating more. Each course and eBook will help you learn why, how, when and where to create and use one specific type of content. Both courses and eBooks are easy to understand, provide actionable steps and advice and include plenty of examples.

To learn more about my courses and eBooks, make sure to visit my "Learn with Me" page online at http://bit.ly/1n6FafB regularly.

Real-Life Content Design Examples

The following two examples tell the story of content design done right. The first is drawn from a post on my www.mattaboutbusiness.com blog while the second shows how I successfully used the example set by the first for my own content.

Real-Life Content Design: Content Design for Engagement

I'm bringing Joe Chernov back to tell another great success story that hinges on a factor many companies miss when they publish PDFs and other documents - content design.

When is a white paper not a white paper? When it's a "Grande Guide" of course! "We wanted to continue to provide value with our white papers," said Chernov. "But at the same time, we wanted to engage the reader with what essentially can be pretty boring stuff."

Chernov and his team started with the setting. He explains, "We asked ourselves, 'Where would folks most like to be when they read our white papers?'" The answer they arrived at was a coffee shop; a spot that brings to mind relaxation while also evoking the sweet buzz of eye-opening caffeine.

These explorations led to the realization that they could use the design of the document as the medium for conveying the setting and tone they were trying to achieve, both of which could lead to better engagement. "When you read in a coffee shop," says Chernov, "You're going to get coffee stains and crumpled paper." The ultimate result was the Grande Guide design as seen in Image 4.17. The name, *Grande* was also pulled from coffee shop nomenclature bringing the design full-circle.

Image 4.17: A Grande Guide

"We wanted to package information in forms that entice people to read them," says Chernov. "The Grande Guide design helped us do just that." Expanding upon the Grande Guide concept, the team created a character named Juan Eloqua who is a coffee bean grower and marketing expert and then featured him in video content. The videos are tongue-in-cheek, but they also provide valuable information while engaging the viewer with an entertaining story.

Chernov and I didn't discuss this, but another benefit I believe they gain from these creative content designs is solid market positioning. They're saying, "We're creative and fun and think out of the box to get it done, not like those stodgy other guys! And we do it all while still providing great info and value!" If I were in the market for the services they provide, I'd choose Eloqua in a heartbeat. The message that comes across to me is that they don't take themselves seriously, but they know their stuff cold. I like both parts of that statement.

Taking a Page From Eloqua's Example

So, where can content design take you? I admit that I was pretty impressed after talking with Joe about the Grande Guide. That lead me to redesign my own free guide, *"The Non-Techie's Guide to Finding and Choosing Software Online"* that I offer at Matt About Business when people sign up for the newsletter (http://bit.ly/1hIjunW).

I went from a plain white background with a target on the front to the guide cover in Image 4.18. It makes me smile and, more importantly, it attracts visitors to sign up for my e-mails years after the change.

Image 4.18: My Redesigned Guide

Before You Move On

Before you move on to chapter 5, here're two handy pieces of advice:

1. Visit http://bit.ly/1nqvV7k to discover helpful and inspirational online resources to use when creating your own content.
2. Use the infographic shown in Image 4.19 as a guide when creating your own content. Follow it and your content will be great!

Bibliography

[1] "Google Hits 67 Percent Market Share Again, Bing Hits Another All-Time High [comScore]," accessed March 11, 2013, http://searchengineland.com/comscore-january-2013-search-rankings-148478

Image 4.19: Follow these guidelines to create great content. Source:
http://bit.ly/1pAK6HZ

Chapter 5: Creating Your Own Content - Start Here

Thus far, I've introduced you to the concepts of content marketing by answering four questions.

1. What is content marketing?
2. Why use content marketing?
3. Is content marketing right for your business?
4. What makes great content?

With the answers to these questions under your belt, it's time think about creating your own online content. Before you get started however, let's talk about some common barriers folks face when they start creating content and discuss how to overcome these hurdles.

The Potential Barriers to Creating Content

The greatest frustration in the field of content marketing is that the key element, content creation, is often the greatest obstacle to success. Why is content creation such an obstacle? Because many business folk get stuck trying to jump over one of these hurdles:

> Ironically, content creation is often the greatest obstacle to content marketing success.

- The stage fright when you think about others reading your posts, listening to your podcasts or watching your videos. It's hard to break through that anxiety to create, and actually publish, your content.

- Believing that you don't have enough time to create content in addition to running your business.
- Feeling overwhelmed by having to learn how to create, and use, certain types of content like videos, podcasts, infographics and more.

Overcoming the Potential Barriers to Creating Content

Let's take a deeper look at these potential barriers and discuss how to overcome them one-by-one.

Stage Fright

Feeling self-conscious about presenting your thoughts to others is common. Many of my clients have equated publishing their own content online with that most dreaded of all things: public speaking. This usually stems from fears like "I'm not creative enough," or "I have nothing new or original to say."

If you can relate to one or both of these, you're not alone. However, you shouldn't let fear stop you from reaping the benefits of content marketing, so let's tackle each one of these fears head on!

"I'm Not Creative Enough"

Let me say this up front – creativity is overrated. Sure, there are amazingly creative people out there and it may seem that you can never get to their level. But, many of the most creative people have a secret weapon that you, as a hard-working person, likely have as well.

That weapon is perseverance.

No one is good at something when they start out. Getting good takes practice and practice means doing it again and again and again. I've learned this from personal experience. I took a fiction writing class in 4 BK (Before Kids) where I heard the saying "Writers write." At the time I was like, "Well duh Captain Obvious, of course they do – that's why we call them writers." But I was young and naive and, as my dreams of being a fiction writer faded into the background of everyday life, I realized just what that phrase meant.

Writers sit down to write when it's time to write.

It doesn't matter if they're in the mood. It doesn't matter if they feel creative. Successful writers put their butt in the chair and grind out word after word. Sometimes it's easy and sometimes it's not, but the job gets done. It gets easier to sit down and get started as time goes on, no matter their mood or what else is going on in their life.

It's happened to me. When I need to create a post, a video, an infographic or some other type of content, my creativity starts to flow when I sit down and start. It doesn't matter if I feel creative when I sit down –a switch is flipped and the more I create, the faster and wider the floodgates open. My friend Marcus Sheridan over at The Sales Lion (www.thesaleslion.com) explains it like this:

"And speaking of "serving garbage on a plate," just look at the first blog articles on my swimming pool site—River Pools. Without question, I served up garbage almost 3 times a week for the first few months of blogging.

I was a bad writer. I was a bad blogger. I was a poor communicator. And nothing was "epic."

But somehow, some way, the "little website that could" is now the most trafficked website in the world for in ground swimming pool construction.

The Sales Lion is no different. I cringe when I go back and read those initial posts on this blog. It's almost like they were written by a different person.

But at the same time, each post was a victory. Each post was a learning experience. And each post was a small rung on the ladder that got me to where I am today (wherever that may be)."

Marcus didn't let his lack of experience stop him – he sat down and gave himself experience. He's also the first person who would tell you that he's not a creative person, but he now turns out post after post of great content. That's because he worked hard, took notes and learned every lesson that came his way, good or bad. He sat his butt in the chair and wrote.

Writer's write. Videographers make videos. Photographers and graphic artists make images and infographics. Radio folks and public speakers create audio. You can do all of those things. You can create online content that appeals to your target markets. Even if you're not a "creative person."

If you want to master the art of creating online content, sit your butt in the chair and create some. It's not to say that you *have* to create your own online content – there are capable creators who can help you and we'll talk more about how to hire them in Appendix A. But if you want to be the voice of your business, if you want to master the art of creating online content, you must sit your butt in the chair and create some.

Again and again and again.

It gets easier, I promise.

I Have Nothing New or Original to Say

I call this the "Me Too Syndrome Blues" or MTSB for short. MTSB hits when you look at the huge amount of existing online content and discover that people are talking about the same things you are. They're having the same conversations you want to have and reaching the same conclusions that you have.

At that moment, an ugly voice in the back of your head asks, "What do I have to contribute to this conversation that's new, interesting or valuable? Why should I create my own content?" You feel discouraged; you feel down. It's a tough moment to be sure and it will arise more than once over your career as a content creator but if you're going to continue on to content marketing success, you have to move past it and keep creating. So what do you do? Here are some ideas I've used to move past MTSB:

Find the Niche Within a Niche

Like the facets on a diamond, every conversation has many sides. When you see other content creators talking about your subject, study their posts and see what topics they're not addressing or points of view they're not exploring. Expand the conversation – every piece of existing content can spawn at least one new piece by taking a throwaway point and making it the center of your piece. Take a high-level conversation and drill down on one point and then another. You'll never run out of things to write about that are interesting, new and of value to your target customers.

Use a Different Type of Content

One of the best things about the Web is that it's not just words; it's images, video and sound, too. If you find that there are lots of people talking about your topics using one type of content, use a different one. People learn and consume information in many different ways. While that nice long blog post over there might make some folks happy, others might want to hear it on their iPod and still others would prefer to watch a video. Try different content types and your audience will find you.

You're a Different Person

Most content creators aren't journalists who must adhere to a code of objectivity. You don't need to keep yourself out of the story. How does this help? By bringing your unique experiences to your readers. Your tone, your outlook, your stories, your beliefs and your opinions all color and enhance your content and make them different and valuable in their own right, even if they cover the same subject as a piece of content that someone else created. You should frame the conversation and tell it your way, from your perspective and in your own voice. For example, I like to write the way I talk. This makes my content conversational and I like the more intimate feeling it gives my readers and me. Next time you feel MTSB sneaking up on you (or ramming into you like a freight train!), try the steps above and chase away those ugly feelings.

I Don't Have Enough Time to Create Content

Time shouldn't stop your content marketing effort. That's because even a little content marketing goes a long way. ***Companies that publish new blog posts just 1-2 times per month generate 70% more leads than companies that don't blog at all.*** [1]

What business wouldn't want 70% more leads? That incredible number demonstrates how achievable content marketing success is for any business. Just 1 or 2 blog posts per month – not per week or day as many experts recommend. That's doable, even for time crunched small business folks. **The takeaway** is that you don't need to launch a huge campaign to start gaining the advantages that content marketing can bring to your business.

Feeling Overwhelmed Learning to Create and Use New Types of Content

I don't blame you! The bad news is that learning how and when to use even the most common types of content such as text, images, videos and e-mail marketing can be downright intimidating. When it comes to the less common types of content like webinars, infographics, podcasts, online radio and mobile apps, many folks just throw-up their hands.

The good news is that I've already created online courses and eBooks for some content types and I'm busily creating more. Each course and eBook will help you learn why, how, when and where to create and use one specific type of content. Both courses and eBooks are easy to understand, provide actionable steps and advice and include plenty of examples. Each one builds on the foundation of knowledge found within this book, and enables you to plan, create and implement increasingly effective content marketing campaigns.

So don't be intimidated by all the different content types and options. Pick one and start there. You can't win a marathon without taking that first step. Grab your beverage of choice, head on over to http://bit.ly/1n6FafB and let's get started learning about the many different types of online content.

I'm waiting for ya'.

> **To stay up-to-date on my latest course and eBook offerings, make sure to visit my "Learn with Me" page online at http://bit.ly/1n6FafB regularly.**

Bibliography

[1] "12 Revealing Charts to Help You Benchmark Your Business Blogging Performance [NEW DATA]," accessed March 13, 2013,

http://blog.hubspot.com/blog/tabid/6307/bid/33742/12-revealing-charts-to-help-you-benchmark-your-business-blogging-performance-new-data

SECTION III: Discover Where You Can Learn More About Content Marketing and Find Help

The aim of the two appendices is to support you as you take your first steps into content marketing. We'll discuss:

1) Why, where and how to hire outside help such as an agency or freelancer, and

2) Where to go online to learn much more about implementing an effective content marketing campaign.

Appendix A – Outside Help: Hiring a Freelancer or Agency

Why Would You Want to Hire Outside Help?

As we discussed in the main body of the book, one of the biggest barriers to executing an effective content marketing program is creating the content. While there are many ways past that barrier (see Chapter 5 for a refresher), sometimes it makes more sense for you to focus on the other parts of your business (you know, that huge pile of non-content marketing to-dos?) rather than devoting energy to content creation.

Even if you have the time and energy to spare, you may not want to create content, and that's just fine. That's right, I'm not gonna' yell at you for feeling that way. Whether it's writing, video editing or any of the other content creation tasks, if you don't like doing it, why torture yourself?

That said, you still want to reap the benefits of content marketing, right? If so, content needs to be created. Who's gonna' create it? Outside resources such as agencies and freelancers, that's who. Believe me, content marketing is hot and there are tons of outside resources ready to jump at the opportunity to help create your posts, videos, infographics and other types of content.

Beyond content creation, you can find help in all aspects of content marketing from strategy to tactics, implementation and measurement. You can use these freelancers to create different types of content and then hire an agency to manage both your overall program and the freelancers. The options are as limitless as your needs (and your pocketbook). In addition, an outside resource that's experienced in content marketing and content creation can move your program along faster than you ever could on your own.

How to Hire Outside Help

Finding the best outside resources, those with the skills and the right fees, can be a chore. However, it's a necessary one if you need help with your content marketing program. There are three ways to find folks to hire.

1. If you already know and trust a freelancer or agency that can handle the work and has the time to do so for the right price, go for it!

2. If you have trustworthy acquaintances who can recommend a freelancer or agency that they know and trust and that resource can handle the work and has the time to do so for the right price, go for it!

3. If neither (1) nor (2) are true, you can find help by visiting an online marketplace. The two I recommend using are Elance and oDesk.

Online Marketplaces

Elance (*http://www.elance.com*)   **oDesk (*http://www.odesk.com*)**

Both Elance and oDesk are large online freelance/agency marketplaces where you can *freely* (for the company that's hiring) post a project, receive multiple bids, award the job to the bidder of your choice, manage the project through completion and pay on an agreed-upon schedule. In other words, you'll save tons of time, energy and money, and avoid a lot of potential frustration, because the entire lifecycle of your project can be handled within a pre-defined, yet flexible, online workflow. Yes, you do not need to reinvent the wheel!

While the two companies merged in December of 2013, the sites will continue to run separately to accommodate the community culture of each. This means that a search for help in both spots is likely to yield different results and may be well worth your time. In addition, while both sites offer very similar features and functionality, they do differ in many small ways. I recommend you test drive both and then go with the one that works the best for you and your business.

Online Marketplaces: Advantages

As I mentioned earlier, there are many advantages to using Elance and/or oDesk to find and hire the content marketing assistance you need. Let's take a closer look at three of the biggest:

Advantages: Detailed Provider Profiles

Using these sites can feel as if you're hiring blind, which is where profiles such as the one in Image A.1 come in handy. Each freelancer/agency profile can provide a lot of useful information such as a resume, a list of standard rates, a portfolio showing past work, a display of ratings in a number of skills (freelancers/agencies can self-rate themselves or they can take online tests to be rated by each site's system) and perhaps most importantly, a display of past buyer ratings and feedback.

I cannot emphasize that last point enough! Ratings and feedback are an excellent way to learn about the people whom you're considering hiring. You'll want to see as many positive ratings as possible, but don't be put off by a few negative ratings among a field of positive. Make sure to look closely at the negative ratings however, especially any feedback comments. If the negatives all seem to be about the type of work you need done, then steer clear.

Image A.1: Part of a freelancer's profile from Elance.

Also, beware of profiles that lack a lot of information. The systems on both sites do not require freelancers/agencies to add more than the basic information to their profile so an incomplete profile may signal that the resource is new which isn't necessarily a bad thing – new often equals less expensive. It may also mean that they're not dedicated enough to the process to spend the time and energy to upgrade their marketability when selling their services which can be a potential sign they may also lack dedication to completing your project competently and on time.

Advantages: Robust Job Posting, Bidding and Award Process

Though the two marketplace sites differ in the details, both Elance and oDesk offer robust job posting, bidding and award systems chock full of features and options.

Robust Job Posting, Bidding and Award Process: 1-2-3 Listing Creation

Posting a job on either marketplace site is as easy as filling out a form such as the one shown in both Images A.2 and A.3. That said, before filling out that form, be sure to spend some time creating clear goals, timelines and deliverables for each project. This will help assure that all potential bidders know what's expected and by when it will need to be delivered.

Once you've nailed down your project details, you can enter them into the form, attach a document that contains more information or do both. One point of note: Elance allows you to "Feature" a job for a small fee. Featured jobs appear at the top the project listings, a fact that increases the odds that providers will notice your listing and submit a bid.

Robust Job Posting, Bidding and Award Process: Job Targeting

Both platforms enable you to adjust the range of targeted providers for each project listing. This range can be as large as the "Public" setting where all providers can view and bid on your project or as small as the "Invited Bids Only" setting where only those providers whom you invite may see the project and submit a bid.

Post a Job

Choose a category	Please select... Please select...
Give your job a title	
Describe the work to be done	
	5000 characters left
What skills are needed?	
How would you like to pay?	Hourly - Pay by the hour. Verify with the Work Diary.
Estimated Duration	Please select...
Estimated Workload	Please select...

Desired Experience Level

ENTRY LEVEL $	INTERMEDIATE $$	EXPERT $$$
I am looking for freelancers with the lowest rates	I am looking for a mix of experience and value	I am willing to pay higher rates for the most experienced freelancers

Marketplace Visibility	Anyone can find this job
Attach a document (optional)	Browse... No file selected. Less than 5MB

Image A.2: The top section of the "Post a Job" form from oDesk.

Customize Your Application Requirements

Preferred Qualifications

Specify the qualifications you're looking for in a successful application. Freelancers may still apply if they do not meet your preferences, but they will be clearly notified that they are at a disadvantage.

Hide Qualifications

Freelancer Type	No preference
Minimum Feedback Score	Any score
Hours Billed on oDesk	Any amount
Location	Any location
English Level (self-assigned)	Any level

Cover Letter

Ask applicants to write a cover letter introducing themselves.

☑ Yes, require a cover letter

Screening Questions

Add a few questions you'd like your candidates to answer when applying to your job.

> What past project or job have you had that is most like this one and why?   ✕

183 characters left

> What challenging part of this job are you most experienced in?   ✕

194 characters left

+ Add Another Question

Preview   Post a Job   Cancel

Image A.3: The bottom section of the "Post a Job" form from oDesk.

Generally, you'll use the "Public" setting when starting out, but as you develop relationships with specific freelancers and agencies, your target range will progressively become smaller until you end up with a group of trusted providers that you invite to bid on each project.

Job Targeting: The Positive Impact on Affordability

A big benefit of these sites is that the open bidding process drives enough competition to drive down your fees, sometimes ridiculously so. Unless price is the sole factor in your selection process, you should keep in mind that the lowest bidder is often not the best bidder in terms of quality and reliability. Be sure to review each bid carefully to assure that the provider is a good fit. This is not to say that price is not important, however; depend on the market to drive it down to an affordable range.

Even after your target narrows to invites only, you can count on the relationship, as well as negotiation, to keep your project fees reasonable.

Robust Job Posting, Bidding and Award Process: Detailed Terms

Both sites include a sophisticated process that records the agreed-upon terms for each project and helps you manage changes (e.g. deliverables, due dates, milestones and fee payouts). These terms become the structure with which you'll manage a project and, more importantly, captures the expectations placed on both parties for the duration of that project.

Robust Job Posting, Bidding and Award Process: Flexible Payment

You can offer providers both fixed-price and hourly-pay terms, either of which can be pre-paid via escrow. Based on the agreed-upon terms, payment can be made at the beginning of a project, when certain milestones are met during the project, at the end of the project or a combination of all three.

In addition, the sites can even handle the 1099 form for your buyers so you don't have to manage that process come tax time. Handy, eh?

Advantages: Project Management

As mentioned previously, on acceptance of a bid, a project's terms becomes a timeline with details such as due dates, deliverables, milestones and fee payouts. In addition to this project calendar, both sites offer:

Project Management: Internal Communication System

Both sites offer an internal communication system that includes e-mails and chats so you can ask questions and talk with providers both during the project's lifetime and after the project is complete. Incidentally, you can use this system to communicate with providers prior to accepting a bid as well. After a bid is accepted, prior conversations become part of the project's history.

Project Management: Project Workspace

Each marketplace offers their own version of a project workspace. Within this workspace you can post documents, view past communications and accept both status reports (if you asked the provider submit them) and timesheets (for hourly-pay projects). This is a great spot for saving versions of your deliverables and the feedback received for each.

Project Management: Project Closure

Lastly, both Elance and oDesk provide a project closure process. If the project went well, this includes the submission of the final deliverables and the payment of the remaining fees. In addition, both you and the provider have the opportunity to provide feedback via both ratings and comments.

If the project did not go well, or even reach completion, a dispute resolution process is available to all parties for each project.

Getting Started

Ready to find the help you need to launch a successful content marketing program? Here are the links you need to get started:

Elance

Website: http://bit.ly/1n60e4a
Help and Support: http://bit.ly/1dlDBl5

oDesk

Website: http://bitly.com/1bE8KlV
Help and Support: http://bitly.com/186tkfb

Appendix B - Online Content Marketing Resource Links Index

This is the spot to be if you want to build on the content marketing knowledge contained in this book. Each of the links below leads to a free, ever-growing list of resources that will help you answer any what, why, how, when and where questions you may have. Yes, that "ever-growing" phrase I threw in there means that it's worth checking the links below on a regular basis because I will continue to add resources as I find them.

A Quick Note About the Web Addresses (URLs) Used in this Book

Many of the links contained in this book were shortened to make them easier for you to use. When entering these links into your browser's address bar, it's important to copy them exactly as they appear in the book using both upper and lower case characters.

Chapter 1 Resources

- **Customer Avatars:** Learn more about creating and using a customer avatar at http://bit.ly/1h3YB0r
- **Calls to Action:** Better understand how to drive customer action using calls to action by visiting http://bit.ly/1hJKGld
- **Test and Measure Your Content Marketing Efforts:** Learn more about these two important topics at http://bit.ly/1eJykKx

Chapter 2 Resources

- **The Benefits of Content Marketing:** To see real life content marketing case studies and success stories, visit http://bit.ly/Wdis9V

Chapter 4 Resources

- **What Makes Great Content?** For how-to resources to use when creating your own content, head on over to http://bit.ly/1nqvV7k

Chapter 5 Resources

- **Creating Your Own Content - Start Here:** If you're looking for some inspiration when you're just getting started with content marketing, visit http://bit.ly/1gB2lar

General Content Marketing Resources

These links lead to resources that I've either created or collected and should prove to be very useful as you begin down the content marketing path:

- **"SEO in Everyday English":** You can find my recorded webinar on search engine optimization at http://bit.ly/1cHUrdO. This is a "must-know" topic for any content marketer.
- **My Content Marketing Pinterest Boards:** I've collected tons of useful content marketing information, mostly in the form of infographics, on my categorized Pinterest boards. Check them out at: http://bit.ly/1mdaMxb

- **The "1000+ Online Content Ideas for Your Business" blog:** come learn more about content marketing on my blog at: http://bit.ly/1qK8lEy
- **The "Content Marketing Small Business Guide":** you'll find a nice collection of useful links in this curated guide to my content marketing articles. Visit http://bit.ly/QpMDs1 to take a look.
- **Learn with Me:** The online gateway to my content marketing courses and eBooks is my "Learn with Me" page at http://bit.ly/1n6FafB

Each course and eBook will help you learn why, how, when and where to create and use one specific type of content. Both courses and eBooks are easy to understand, provide actionable steps and advice and include plenty of examples. Each one builds on the foundation of knowledge found within this book, and enables you to plan, create and implement increasingly effective content marketing campaigns.

INDEX

ABOUT THE AUTHOR

Matt Mansfield is the President of Matt About Business where he helps entrepreneurs and Fortune 500 companies create powerful content that drives targeted online traffic month-after-month. You can see examples of his content work

by visiting his portfolio site at: http://www.mattsmansfield.com.

A published author, Matt's contributions have been featured on sites such as the American Express OPEN Forum, the SCORE Small Business Blog and Pitney Bowes' pbSmart™ Essentials blog as well as many others (view links to my published content at http://bit.ly/1j0sOik).

Matt also writes about small business topics over at the Matt About Business blog (http://www.mattaboutbusiness.com) and about content marketing on the 1000+ Online Content Ideas for Your Business blog (http://www.1000contentideas.com) so come on by and say, "Hi!"

A dedicated content marketing evangelist, Matt is busily adding to a growing number of online courses and eBooks, each of which will help you learn why, how, when and where to create and use one specific type of content. Learn more at: http://bit.ly/1n6FafB.

Matt lives in the suburbs North of Chicago with his wife, four kids, one dog, three fish and many, many books.

Made in the USA
Charleston, SC
06 August 2014